Can Renewable Energy Replace Fossil Fuels?

Hal Marcovitz

INCONTROVERSY

ReferencePoint Press®

San Diego, CA

© 2011 ReferencePoint Press, Inc.

For more information, contact:
ReferencePoint Press, Inc.
PO Box 27779
San Diego, CA 92198
www.ReferencePointPress.com

Picture credits:
Cover: iStockphoto.com
Maury Aaseng: 17
AP Images: 9, 15, 44, 54, 56, 63, 73, 76
Photos.com: 19, 20, 24, 32, 37, 41
Science Photo Library: 7

LIBRARY OF CONGRESS CATALOGING-IN-PUBLICATION DATA

Marcovitz, Hal.
  Can renewable energy replace fossil fuels? / by Hal Marcovitz.
    p. cm. — (In controversy)
  Includes bibliographical references and index.
  ISBN-13: 978-1-60152-113-2 (hardback)
  ISBN-10: 1-60152-113-8 (hardback)
  1. Renewable energy sources—Juvenile literature. 2. Fossil fuels—Juvenile literature. I. Title.
  TJ808.2.M365 2011
  333.79'4—dc22
                                                          2009050482

Contents

Foreword

n 2008, as the U.S. economy and economies worldwide were falling into the worst recession since the Great Depression, most Americans had difficulty comprehending the complexity, magnitude, and scope of what was happening. As is often the case with a complex, controversial issue such as this historic global economic recession, looking at the problem as a whole can be overwhelming and often does not lead to understanding. One way to better comprehend such a large issue or event is to break it into smaller parts. The intricacies of global economic recession may be difficult to understand, but one can gain insight by instead beginning with an individual contributing factor such as the real estate market. When examined through a narrower lens, complex issues become clearer and easier to evaluate.

This is the idea behind ReferencePoint Press's *In Controversy* series. The series examines the complex, controversial issues of the day by breaking them into smaller pieces. Rather than looking at the stem cell research debate as a whole, a title would examine an important aspect of the debate such as *Is Stem Cell Research Necessary?* or *Is Embryonic Stem Cell Research Ethical?* By studying the central issues of the debate individually, researchers gain a more solid and focused understanding of the topic as a whole.

Each book in the series provides a clear, insightful discussion of the issues, integrating facts and a variety of contrasting opinions for a solid, balanced perspective. Personal accounts and direct quotes from academic and professional experts, advocacy groups, politicians, and others enhance the narrative. Sidebars add depth to the discussion by expanding on important ideas and events. For quick reference, a list of key facts concludes every chapter. Source notes, an annotated organizations list, bibliography, and index provide student researchers with additional tools for papers and class discussion.

The *In Controversy* series also challenges students to think critically about issues, to improve their problem-solving skills, and to sharpen their ability to form educated opinions. As President Barack Obama stated in a March 2009 speech, success in the twenty-first century will not be measurable merely by students' ability to "fill in a bubble on a test but whether they possess 21st century skills like problem-solving and critical thinking and entrepreneurship and creativity." Those who possess these skills will have a strong foundation for whatever lies ahead.

No one can know for certain what sort of world awaits today's students. What we can assume, however, is that those who are inquisitive about a wide range of issues; open-minded to divergent views; aware of bias and opinion; and able to reason, reflect, and reconsider will be best prepared for the future. As the international development organization Oxfam notes, "Today's young people will grow up to be the citizens of the future: but what that future holds for them is uncertain. We can be quite confident, however, that they will be faced with decisions about a wide range of issues on which people have differing, contradictory views. If they are to develop as global citizens all young people should have the opportunity to engage with these controversial issues."

In Controversy helps today's students better prepare for tomorrow. An understanding of the complex issues that drive our world and the ability to think critically about them are essential components of contributing, competing, and succeeding in the twenty-first century.

The Consequences of Fossil Fuel Use

Coal is a fossil fuel, meaning it is composed of the remnants of trees and plants that have been buried under tremendous pressure for millions of years. It is not renewable—once the coal is dug out of the ground and burned, it cannot be replaced. Moreover, burned coal leaves toxic waste behind—ash that contains high concentrations of mercury, selenium, arsenic, lead, and other hazardous materials. All that coal ash has to be stored somewhere. In America power companies, which burn coal to make electricity, have been getting rid of the ash by submerging it in ponds.

For years the Tennessee Valley Authority, which supplies energy to portions of seven southern states, dumped 1,000 tons (907 metric tons) of coal ash a day into an 84-acre pond (34ha) near Kingston, Tennessee. Surrounding the pond was a wall composed of compacted earth. In late 2008 the pond's earthen wall broke; an estimated 1 billion gallons (3.8 billion L) of coal ash sludge poured into the town, swamping homes and businesses and fouling the nearby Emory River.

Although the U.S. Environmental Protection Agency (EPA) has conducted a cleanup and trucked tons of coal ash away to be dumped in a toxic landfill in Alabama, Kingston soon became almost a ghost town—most of the residents left their homes, fearing the health consequences of living in an environment coated with the remnants of toxic waste. "There are huge health concerns," says Kingston resident Deanna Copeland. "It's going to

"There are huge health concerns. It's going to get in our house. We're going to breathe it in. It would be like walking through a dust bowl, and we don't know what's in the dust."[1]

— Deanna Copeland, a resident of Kingston, Tennessee.

get in our house. We're going to breathe it in. It would be like walking through a dust bowl, and we don't know what's in the dust."[1]

Accidents involving fossil fuels, which also include oil and natural gas, have occurred before. In 1989 the huge tanker *Exxon Valdez* struck a reef in Prince William Sound in Alaska, spilling some 11 million gallons (41.6 million L) of crude oil into the waterway. The oily muck fouled the shoreline and rocky coves of the sound, polluting wildlife habitats. Twenty years after the spill, scientific tests have indicated that habitats for the wildlife in the sound have still not recovered from the accident.

Even so, the most pressing issue involving fossil fuels centers on their emissions of so-called greenhouse gases, which contribute to climate change. Environmentalists believe there is no greater threat to the ecology of the Earth than emissions of carbon dioxide and similar gases, which are already regarded as responsible for raising the Earth's temperature. Unless alternatives are found, environmental experts predict dire consequences for the planet—the melting of the polar ice caps, a rise in ocean temperature, the loss

Accidents involving fossil fuels can be devastating. Wildlife habitats in Alaska's Prince William Sound still have not recovered from the 1989 Exxon Valdez *oil spill. In this photo, workers use high-pressure hot water hoses to clean up spilled oil after the tanker struck a reef.*

of species, and severe storms, among other problems. Says James Hansen, the director of the Goddard Institute for Space Studies, which monitors global warming, "This particular problem has become an emergency."[2]

"An Irreversible Catastrophe"

There are alternatives to fossil fuels—so-called renewable energy sources that provide energy while not emitting greenhouse gases or other forms of pollution. Among these resources are solar power, wind power, and geothermal power, which provides energy drawn from the earth's own heat. These energy sources have widespread support among Americans. A 2008 poll by the Washington, D.C.–based Pew Research Center found that 76 percent of Americans support expanded use of renewable energy as a way to stem climate change. Says U.S. president Barack Obama: "Our generation's response to this challenge will be judged by history, for if we fail to meet it—boldly, swiftly, and together—we risk consigning future generations to an irreversible catastrophe . . . And the time we have to reverse this tide is running out."[3]

And yet questions have been raised about whether renewable energy resources can adequately replace fossil fuels. Critics argue that the establishment of solar, wind, and other renewable energy programs would cost billions of dollars; moreover, they suggest that even if Americans make a commitment to renewable energy, not enough renewable energy resources exist to fuel the needs of Americans. They urge lawmakers not to abandon fossil fuels. "There's no reason why we can't dramatically increase our use of coal while still protecting the environment," argues Newt Gingrich, a former Speaker of the U.S. House of Representatives and a possible candidate for president in 2012. "We have the coal resources to solve our energy crisis and are developing energy technology to use it cleanly."[4]

Long-Lasting Environmental Damage

If, as Gingrich suggests, it is possible to develop clean coal technology, the advancement would come too late to help the residents of

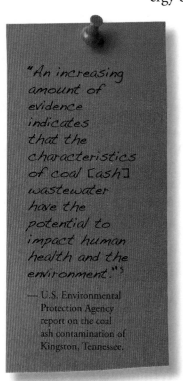

"An increasing amount of evidence indicates that the characteristics of coal [ash] wastewater have the potential to impact human health and the environment."[5]

— U.S. Environmental Protection Agency report on the coal ash contamination of Kingston, Tennessee.

Kingston. In late 2009 the EPA issued a report confirming what many in Kingston had suspected: the ash spill caused severe and lasting damage to the environment. Said the EPA report:

> An increasing amount of evidence indicates that the characteristics of coal [ash] wastewater have the potential to impact human health and the environment. Many of the common pollutants found in coal [ash] wastewater (selenium, mercury, and arsenic) are known to cause environmental harm and can potentially represent a human health risk. Pollutants in coal [ash] wastewater are of particular concern because they can occur in large quantities and at high concentrations. . . . In addition, some pollutants in coal [ash] wastewater present an increased ecological threat due to their tendency to persist in the environment and accumulate in organisms, which often results in slow ecological recovery times following exposure.[5]

An estimated billion gallons of coal ash sludge poured into Kingston, Tennessee, in 2008 after a storage pond wall collapsed. The spill destroyed homes (pictured) and businesses and fouled wildlife habitat in and around the nearby Emory River.

Added Leo Francendese, an EPA official dispatched to Kingston to supervise the cleanup: "In the wrong circumstances, coal ash is dangerous. Breathing it, that's dangerous."[6]

The coal ash spill in Tennessee illustrates the enormous environmental concerns of using fossil fuels and how long it often takes to clean up the mess. A year after the spill, the EPA had managed to clean up less than a quarter of the ash that swamped the town and river. Certainly, the long-lasting environmental damage caused by the *Exxon Valdez* spill provides proof that once fossil fuels foul the environment, things may never return to normal. As for the people of Kingston, it may be quite some time before the residents return to their homes if, in fact, they do choose to go home.

Facts

- Before the coal ash broke through its containment pond near Kingston, Tennessee, the ash had accumulated into a "waste cake" that was 60 feet (18.3m) thick.

- If the coal ash spilled near Kingston were spread out evenly, it would create a 1-foot layer of sludge (30.5cm) over an area of 3,000 acres (1,214ha).

- Of the three fossil fuels, coal emits the most greenhouse gases. When burned, coal emits 70 percent more greenhouse gases than natural gas and 25 percent more greenhouse gases than oil.

What Are the Origins of the Controversy over Fossil Fuels?

The numbers would seem to suggest that reserves of fossil fuels are virtually inexhaustible. According to the London, England–based World Energy Council, there are more than 800 billion tons (725 billion metric tons) of coal, 1.2 trillion barrels of crude oil, and 235 trillion cubic yards (180 trillion cu. m) of natural gas still available beneath the surface of the earth. Experts agree that reserves of fossil fuels will be available for the duration of the twenty-first century and most likely well beyond. "Humans will have at our disposal as much gasoline as we can burn in the 21st century," says author and energy expert Mark Hertsgaard. "Nor are we likely to run out of heating oil, coal or natural gas, the other carbon-based fuels that have powered industrial civilization for 200 years."[7]

The three major fossil fuels are oil, coal, and natural gas, which is composed mostly of methane. Getting them out of the earth requires considerable engineering prowess—coal must be mined, either in deep mines that burrow thousands of feet into the earth, or in surface-mining operations that strip the coal away from mountainsides. To extract oil and natural gas from the earth, deep holes must be drilled into the planet. Some of the deepest oil wells can be found under offshore drilling platforms in the Gulf of

Mexico, where engineers have drilled 4 miles (6.4km) below the ocean floor.

Without fossil fuels, the economies of America and all other industrialized countries would quickly grind to a halt. Oil provides gasoline for cars and diesel fuel for trucks as well as heating fuel for many homes. Oil is also an important ingredient of plastic, meaning that it is used in the manufacture of thousands of products. Natural gas is used for home heating and industrial purposes. Coal has a long history of use in America—it is believed the Hopi Indians of the Southwest started using coal for cooking, heating, and making pottery as far back as the 1300s. By the 1800s coal was employed to heat buildings, provide energy for factories, and fire the engines of locomotives. Today most buildings are no longer heated by coal, most trains run on electricity, and most factories use other forms of energy as well. Still, coal remains an important energy source. It is widely used to make electricity—coal-fired plants generate about half the electricity used in America today.

Fossil fuels also emit greenhouse gases, most notably carbon dioxide, that contribute to climate change. According to the Intergovernmental Panel on Climate Change (IPCC), an organization created by the United Nations Environment Programme and the World Meteorological Organization, if fossil fuel use continues at its current pace, the planet's temperature could rise by as much as 11.5°F (6.4°C) by the end of the twenty-first century. The IPCC drew its conclusions after assessing the research of more than 2,000 scientific studies.

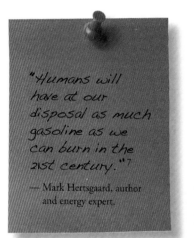

"Humans will have at our disposal as much gasoline as we can burn in the 21st century."[7]

— Mark Hertsgaard, author and energy expert.

The Greenhouse Effect

The notion that the Earth's temperature is rising due to the burning of fossil fuels was first raised in 1896 by Swedish physicist Svante Arrhenius, who suggested that carbon dioxide and similar gases trap heat in the atmosphere and reflect it back to Earth. Arrhenius coined the term *greenhouse effect* because in a greenhouse the sun shines through the clear panes of glass, where it heats the air inside and enables plants to grow even though the outside temperature may be very cold. In a greenhouse most of the heat does

Global Warming Skeptics

There are skeptics who suggest that global warming is much ado about nothing. They argue that warming and cooling cycles are normal and have occurred on the surface of the Earth since the earliest days of the planet. They point to re-occurrences of ice ages approximately every 100,000 years. During such periods great sheets of ice cover much of the Northern Hemisphere but disappear as the Earth warms.

Further, some suggest that carbon dioxide is a gas that occurs naturally in the environment—it is, after all, emitted by people and animals when they exhale—and therefore should be of little concern. Argues Danish environmental writer Bjorn Lomborg, "Global warming, though its size and future projections are rather unrealistically pessimistic, is almost certainly taking place . . . but the typical cure of early and radical fossil fuel cutbacks is way worse than the original affliction and, moreover, its total impact will not pose a devastating problem for our future."

Quoted in Ben Wattenberg, *Fewer: How the New Demography of Depopulation Will Shape Our Future.* Chicago: Ivan R. Dee, 2004, p. 152.

not escape through the glass panes, because it has been absorbed by the plants. In the greenhouse effect described by Arrhenius, the carbon dioxide and other gases in the atmosphere trap the heat, which is absorbed by the oceans and terrain of the Earth.

In 1951 Guy Stewart Callendar of Great Britain published a paper asserting that the carbon dioxide content of the Earth's atmosphere had increased by 10 percent since the 1890s. Callendar was not a scientist—he was an engineer who specialized in steam power. Nevertheless, his findings prompted others with expertise in chemistry, meteorology, and similar sciences to begin taking a hard look at the issue of climate change. Over the next few decades, several scientists produced studies supporting the theory that the Earth's temperature is rising, and in 1979 the National

Academy of Sciences issued a report confirming that global warming is a consequence of fossil fuel use.

A 2007 report by the IPCC provided further proof, finding that the years 1995 through 2006 included some of the warmest on record, dating back to 1850. In the century between 1907 and 2007, the IPCC concluded, the average temperature of the Earth climbed by 1.44°F, or 0.8°C. These numbers may seem minor, but according to the IPCC, the greenhouse effect has already led to environmental change—the average temperature in the Arctic has risen twice the global average during the past 100 years. This means that in recent years the polar ice cap has been melting at a fast rate. Since 1978, the IPCC found, the size of the Arctic ice cap has shrunk by 3.3 percent. "Warming of the climate system is unequivocal, as is now evident from observations of increases in global average air and ocean temperatures, widespread melting of snow and ice and rising global average sea level,"[8] says a 2007 report by the IPCC.

This rise in temperature would mean far graver circumstances than simply more agreeable winters in places like Minnesota and Montana. It is believed that global warming could have horrific environmental consequences, including devastating droughts and floods as well as shrinking glaciers, rising sea levels, and loss of many species. Already, the harshness of some storms has been blamed on the climate change that has already occurred since fossil fuels first went into widespread use more than a century ago. Says Obama:

> No nation, however large or small, wealthy or poor, can escape the impact of climate change. Rising sea levels threaten every coastline. More powerful storms and floods threaten every continent. More frequent droughts and crop failures breed hunger and conflict in places where hunger and conflict already thrive. On shrinking islands, families are already being forced to flee their homes as climate refugees. The security and stability of each nation and all peoples—our prosperity, our health, and our safety—are in jeopardy.[9]

Hostile Regimes

In addition to the environmental risks of continuing to use fossil fuels, the United States and other nations often find themselves relying on unstable and sometimes even hostile regimes to provide oil. The United States imports oil from Venezuela even though the country's president, Hugo Chávez, has emerged as a major critic of America. For years Libya was on the list of nations regarded as supporters of terrorism; only after Libyan leader Muammar al-Qadhafi renounced terrorism and ended his country's weapons of mass destruction program did the United States resume buying oil from Libya. Before the Iraq War deposed dictator Saddam Hussein in 2003, the United States refused to buy oil from the Iraqis. Likewise, oil exporter Angola has only recently returned to a stable democracy after decades of civil war. Russia is a major supplier of oil to the United States despite occasional frosty relations between the two countries.

Even "friendly" oil exporters raise concerns. The Saudis are dedicated allies in the Middle East, but their regime is held in low regard by human rights activists, particularly because women are denied equal rights in the conservative Muslim nation. Says a U.S. Department of State report:

> Despite generally good relations, the United States remains concerned about human rights conditions in Saudi Arabia. Principal human rights issues include abuse of prisoners and incommunicado detention; prohibitions or severe restrictions on freedom of speech, press, peaceful assembly

Scientists warn that the burning of fossil fuels hastens climate change. A dramatic sign of climate change can be seen at Glacier National Park in Montana, where photos taken in 1938, 1981, 1998, and 2005 (from left to right) show Grinnell Glacier receding and the lake below it growing.

and association, and religion; denial of the right of citizens to change their government; systematic discrimination against women and ethnic and religious minorities; and suppression of workers' rights.[10]

It was the hostility of oil-producing nations in the Middle East toward America that first prompted the drive toward renewable resources. In 1973 two Arab states—Egypt and Syria—launched an offensive against Israel in an attempt to regain territory those nations had lost to Israel in an earlier conflict. The attack against the Israelis occurred on Yom Kippur, the most solemn holiday on the Jewish calendar. The Israelis were not caught unprepared, though, and after a week of heavy fighting, they were able to repel the invading armies and drive farther into Arab territory. This victory was in no small measure due to the decision by U.S. president Richard Nixon to resupply the Israeli army with arms and ammunition. The conflict, which came to be known as the Yom Kippur War, ended after three weeks with the Arab armies in retreat.

The Egyptians and Syrians were backed by a number of Arab oil-producing states in the Middle East, most notably Saudi Arabia. Angry with the Americans for aiding the Israelis, the Saudis declared an embargo on oil shipments to the United States. Other Arab oil producers joined in the embargo. For six months the Arab oil-producing nations withheld crude oil from American oil companies. Back in America drivers found themselves waiting in long lines, sometimes for hours, to buy a tank of gasoline. Meanwhile, with demand high and supplies low, the price of a gallon of gas skyrocketed. Prior to the embargo, gasoline had been cheap—selling for 30 to 40 cents a gallon—but during the embargo the price nearly doubled. The embargo finally ended in March 1974 when Secretary of State Henry Kissinger was able to negotiate a cease-fire and an Israeli pullback from Arab territories. But the price of gasoline never went back to its preembargo levels and, in fact, has continued to escalate. By the summer of 2008 the price of gasoline had reached well over $4 a gallon in some parts of the United States.

"Warming of the climate system is unequivocal, as is now evident from observations of increases in global average air and ocean temperatures, widespread melting of snow and ice and rising global average sea level."[8]

— Intergovernmental Panel on Climate Change.

The Climate Is Changing

Recent decades have seen an increase in the Earth's average surface temperature, a rise in its average sea level, and a decrease in snow cover in the Northern Hemisphere. Most scientists believe these changes are the result of human activity. A small group believes they have occurred naturally.

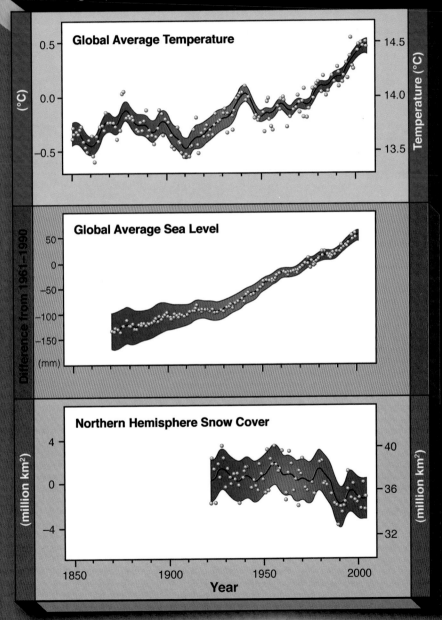

Source: Intergovernmental Panel on Climate Change, "Climate Change 2007: Summary for Policymakers," 2007, pp. 5, 19. www.ipcc.ch.

"Crisis Inspires Change"

The oil embargo occurred during an era in which Americans as well as citizens of other nations had awakened to the realities of pollution. The first Earth Day was staged in 1970. This is an annual celebration that calls attention to the value of the Earth's environment. Also in 1970, Congress adopted major revisions to the Clean Air Act, first adopted in the 1950s, that set tough new standards to reduce air pollution. In 1972 the U.S. Environmental Protection Agency set new gasoline emissions standards that required oil companies to produce gasoline without lead, a toxic metal. As part of this movement, many energy experts started looking toward the viability of replacing fossil fuels with renewable resources. "Crisis inspires change," says Bernard J. Bulkin, an author and expert on renewable energy. "In 1973, the oil embargo associated with the Yom Kippur War led many people to look at the technologies around energy and predict that radical change would occur."[11]

Of course, there was nothing really radical about many forms of renewable energy. People had been using sun power, wind power, and similar renewable resources routinely for many years. People who hang their laundry on a clothesline use the power of the sun, rather than an electric or gas dryer, to dry their clothes. For centuries windmills have been a quaint and familiar sight across the Netherlands; they employ the power of the wind to grind the grain inside the mill. The technique of damming rivers to create hydroelectric power was nearly a century old by the time of the oil embargo. During the 1960s and 1970s, the American space program achieved many technological marvels—most notably the moon landing in 1969. Many people followed the missions to the moon during that era, but relatively few noticed that the energy for America's spacecraft was provided by sunlight absorbed by flat panels that captured the radiation of the sun and converted it into electricity.

The science behind solar energy dates back to 1876 when William Grylls Adams, a British college professor, discovered that the metallic element selenium produced electricity when it was struck by sunlight. This phenomenon is known as the photoelectric effect. In the 1950s scientists at Bell Laboratories in New Jersey developed the first solar collectors, which were able to gather energy from the sun and convert it into electricity.

Indeed, when people think of solar energy, they envision photovoltaic, or PV, collectors attached to people's roofs. That is often the case, but there are also vast "solar farms" providing energy to thousands of homes. By 2011 the world's largest solar farm will be operating near Deming, New Mexico, where solar panels will be spread over a 3,200 acre (1,295ha) property, supplying enough power for 240,000 homes. Solar power can also be effective on a much smaller scale; in Kenya tens of thousands of homes are powered by inexpensive solar systems that generate enough electricity to provide light and operate appliances in the average, modest Kenyan home.

Another way in which solar energy provides power to people's homes is through the solar thermal process. As with the photovoltaic process, solar thermal employs collectors mounted on rooftops. In this case, though, a fluid flowing through the collectors is heated, then pumped into the home, where it passes through a heat exchanger, which is a device that collects the heat from the fluid and transfers it to the home. The fluid most often used is glycol, which is a vegetable-based product that will not freeze in cold weather. Most solar thermal systems are used to heat the water in hot water tanks.

Solar farms, similar to the one pictured here, provide power to large and small communities around the world. The world's largest solar farm, planned for operation in Deming, New Mexico, will cover 3,200 acres and supply enough power for 240,000 homes.

Wind and Biomass

Over the years there have been many other advancements in the development of renewable energy sources that have made them practical as well as available for use on a widespread basis. For example, Germany, Spain, and Denmark are leaders in making use of wind power. Visitors to those countries can see their mountainous landscapes dotted with wind turbines, making use of the strong air currents that sweep across the European continent. In fact, the northern German state of Schleswig-Holstein meets a quarter of its annual electricity demand through wind power; more than 2,400 wind turbines dominate the local landscape.

Germany, Spain, and Denmark lead the world in wind power. Wind turbines similar to those pictured here make use of strong air currents that sweep across the European continent.

Biomass is the use of organic matter to produce energy. These sources can include wood and plants but also manure and garbage. These are renewable sources because new plants and trees can grow to replace those that have been used to provide fuel. Essentially, any Boy Scout or Girl Scout who has built a campfire to provide warmth as well as a source of heat for cooking has made use of biomass energy. However, biomass can be employed on a much larger scale. Some industrial facilities have found they can meet their energy needs by burning wood, bark, sawdust, wood chips, and wood scraps. Some homeowners have installed wood-burning stoves that help heat their homes, although in most cases, the stoves do not provide all the power and homeowners rely on backup electric, oil, or gas systems.

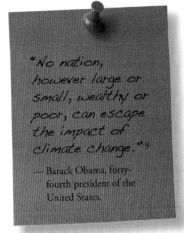

"No nation, however large or small, wealthy or poor, can escape the impact of climate change."[9]

— Barack Obama, forty-fourth president of the United States.

Another form of biomass is "waste to energy." Technically, biomass waste includes organic materials only, such as lawn clippings, food scraps, and leaves. But with the exception of occasional leaf or yard-waste collections, most communities do not provide regular curbside collections in which organic waste is separated from household trash. As such, trash is often included as a biomass product and is burned in waste-to-energy plants. There are about 90 waste-to-energy plants in the United States that use trash as fuel for incinerators that produce steam, which in turn provides energy to turbines that make electricity. These plants provide electricity to some 3 million homes in America.

In America renewable energy can even be found at gasoline pumps. In 1980, Congress passed a law providing incentives to manufacturers to build plants for processing farm crops into ethanol. Also known as ethyl alcohol, ethanol is a form of biomass fuel—it is refined from corn, sugarcane, and similar crops. Soon after the law was adopted, ethanol became an ingredient in automotive fuel and today 10 percent of the fuel pumped into automobile gas tanks is composed of ethyl alcohol.

In fact, ethanol has a history of use in America as an automotive fuel that dates back to the earliest days of the automobile. Nearly a century ago, when the American car industry was in its infancy, there were few oil refineries that converted crude oil into

What Are the Greenhouse Gases?

Carbon dioxide is regarded as the most common of the greenhouse gases, but there are five others. Carbon dioxide and two other gases—methane and nitrous oxide—occur naturally in the environment. Methane is a chief component of natural gas, which is a fossil fuel found beneath the surface of the earth and a product of the breakdown of organic waste such as landfills and manure. Nitrous oxide is familiar to many people who are afraid of the dentist's drill. Nitrous oxide—often known as laughing gas—is not really a painkiller, but when the gas is inhaled, it provides a feeling of euphoria in the patient, enabling him or her to undergo the procedure without fear.

Three other greenhouse gases are not found in the natural environment and instead are manufactured for industrial uses. These include hydrofluorocarbons, perfluorocarbons, and sulfur hexafluoride. Hydrofluorocarbons are used as components in refrigerants and aerosol cans and are hundreds of times more effective in trapping heat in the atmosphere than carbon dioxide. Therefore, every time somebody uses an aerosol can to paint or to use hair spray, he or she is adding a chemical to the atmosphere that promotes climate change.

Perfluorocarbons are employed in the manufacture of electronic components. Sulfur hexafluoride has a number of industrial uses, including the manufacture of electronic components and as a filler gas for windows that feature double panes.

gasoline. As such, car makers did not believe gasoline would be a viable fuel and instead searched for a readily available fuel that could power an internal combustion engine. They soon focused on ethyl alcohol, which is the key ingredient of alcoholic beverages—certainly, a substance that could be found in ample supply. One of the first cars manufactured by the Ford Motor Company ran entirely on ethyl alcohol—fuel that would have otherwise gone into the production of beer and liquor. In 1916, Henry Ford, the company's founder, said, "All the world is waiting for a substitute for gasoline. The day is not far distant when, for every one of those barrels of gasoline, a barrel of alcohol must be substituted."[12] Eventually, though, as gasoline became available, the car companies dropped their plans to use ethanol and engineered their vehicles to run on fossil fuels.

Damming Rivers and Tapping Geothermal Energy

Anybody who has visited a dammed river has witnessed the awesome capability of hydropower. Hydropower is simply using the power of running water to create energy. That is why the early settlers built their grain mills next to flowing streams—so that the waterwheels could turn the millstones inside the mill. On a larger scale, engineers have been damming rivers and forcing the water to spin turbine blades since 1882 with the damming of the Fox River near Appleton, Wisconsin. Now hydroelectric plants create about 6 percent of the electricity consumed in America. The Grand Coulee Dam on the Columbia River in the state of Washington is the country's largest hydroelectric generator—it provides power to people in 11 states, sending electricity as far south as Los Angeles, California, and as far east as Chicago, Illinois. Sixty percent of the electricity used in Spokane, Washington, a city of some 200,000 people, is supplied by the Grand Coulee Dam.

Another form of renewable energy is geothermal power, which is heat generated by the Earth's core. Natural examples of geothermal energy include volcanoes, geysers, and hot springs. More practically, engineers pump water into hot spots deep underground, then make use of the steam that emerges to drive turbines and make energy. Another type of geothermal energy plant feeds the steam into a heat exchanger, which transfers the heat to another liquid that drives the turbines. Homeowners can install geothermal heat pumps for their homes. Even though the surface of the ground may be below freezing, the temperature just 10 feet (3m)

"Crisis inspires change. In 1973, the oil embargo associated with the Yom Kippur War led many people to look at the technologies around energy and predict that radical change would occur."[11]

— Bernard J. Bulkin, author and expert on renewable energy.

Washington State's Grand Coulee Dam (pictured) is the largest hydroelectric generator in the United States. It provides power to 11 states, including parts of California and Illinois.

below the surface stays constant at 50°F to 60°F (10°C to 15.6°C). Geothermal heat pumps use the temperature of the soil to warm homes and buildings in the winter and cool them in the summer.

From putting solar collectors on their roofs to making use of electricity generated by hydropower, there are many steps people can take to cut down on their use of fossil fuels. Many of those technologies have their roots in the 1973 Arab oil embargo—a time when scientists and engineers responded to a crisis and found ways to make people less reliant on fuels provided by unfriendly regimes. Now most scientists are in agreement that climate change represents a new crisis, and once again people will be challenged to find ways to live without fossil fuels.

Facts

- Warming of the oceans has been occurring at depths as low as 9,800 feet (3,000m); it is believed the oceans absorb 80 percent of the heat reflected back by greenhouses gases.

- The rate of increase in the atmosphere of three greenhouse gases—carbon dioxide, methane, and nitrous oxide—was higher during the past 100 years than at any other time in the past 10,000 years.

- Methane is considered 22 times more effective in reflecting the sun's radiation than carbon dioxide.

- Because of an expected increased use of fossil fuels in the near future, carbon dioxide emissions are anticipated to grow between 40 and 110 percent by 2030.

- In 2004 geologists for the oil company Chevron Corporation announced they had located a section of the ocean floor in the Gulf of Mexico containing up to 15 billion barrels of crude oil.

- According to the Intergovernmental Panel on Climate Change, sea levels could rise by 20 inches (50cm) or more by the end of the twenty-first century—that could be a particular concern for Americans, since half the population of the United States lives within 50 miles (80km) of the country's coastlines.

- The ancient Greeks were the first to make use of solar energy; whenever possible, they built their homes so they would face the sun in the winter.

CHAPTER TWO

How Practical Is Renewable Energy?

As the American economy stumbled through the recession of 2009, the country's troubled automobile dealerships found themselves with an unlikely windfall. In just a two-month period, American auto dealers sold some 700,000 new cars, thanks to a $3 billion voucher program funded by the federal government. Under the program the owners of old cars could get vouchers of up to $4,500 from the federal government to be used toward the purchase of new cars if they traded in their gas guzzlers. These are vehicles judged by the U.S. Environmental Protection Agency to be low in fuel efficiency. The official name for the program was the Car Allowance Rebate System (CARS), but it soon became known by its more familiar nickname: Cash for Clunkers.

Although there is no question that Cash for Clunkers provided much-needed aid for the financially ailing dealerships as well as the makers of the cars, the program had a much wider purpose: to get old, gas-guzzling vehicles off the road and replace them with newer, fuel-efficient models. In fact, the size of the voucher depended on the fuel efficiency of the new car. In Philadelphia, Thomas Raiker owned his Lincoln Continental for nearly 15 years, putting some 140,000 miles (225,308km) on the odometer. The car is a huge vehicle that, when new, averaged just 17 miles per gallon (7.23km/L) in city driving. Now, 15 years later, its fuel efficiency was believed to be considerably less, easily below 10 miles per gallon (4.25km/L). Raiker took advantage of the Cash for Clunkers program to trade in the Continental for a much smaller car, the

Chevrolet Aveo, which is rated at 27 miles per gallon (11.5km/L) in city driving. "I'm very happy and relieved,"[13] Raiker said soon after making the deal. As for Raiker's old Continental, the dealership was prohibited under law from selling it to a new owner. Under the terms of the program, it had to be scrapped.

Car dealers may have welcomed the program, but critics found that it had far less of an impact on fossil fuel use in America. Christopher Knittle, an economics professor at the University of California, Davis, calculated that the program would help save about 270 gallons (1,022L) of gasoline per car per year. Knittle said that translates to a savings of about 12,000 barrels of oil a day—which sounds significant, until one realizes that cars owned by Americans burn through 9 million barrels of oil a day. "It really is just a drop in the bucket in terms of gasoline consumption," said Knittle. "Within the U.S. there are about 250 million cars on the road. When we are playing around with only 700,000, it is hard to get any large impact."[14]

The Cash for Clunkers program illustrated that while efforts to reduce reliance on fossil fuels are often made with the best intentions, many of those efforts ultimately have minimal impacts on the use of oil, gas, and coal. Indeed, so much of the world economy is based on the consumption of fossil fuels that many critics believe that, at this juncture, it is impractical to expect the use of renewable energy sources to have much more than a minimal impact on fossil fuel consumption. Says Robert L. Bradley Jr., president of the Texas-based Institute for Energy Research:

> Renewable energy—power generated from the nearly infinite elements of nature such as sunshine, wind, the movement of water, the internal heat of the Earth, and the combustion of replenishable crops—is widely popular with the public and governmental officials because it is thought to be an inexhaustible and environmentally benign source of power, particularly compared with the supposedly finite and environmentally problematic alternative of reliance on fossil fuels. . . . Yet all renewable energy sources

"The list of renewable fuels that were once promising but are now being questioned on economic or environmental grounds, or both, is growing."[15]

—Robert L. Bradley Jr., president of the Texas-based Institute for Energy Research.

are not created equal. Some are more economically and environmentally viable than others. The list of renewable fuels that were once promising but are now being questioned on economic or environmental grounds, or both, is growing.[15]

Commitments to Solar Energy

The Cash for Clunkers program was sparked by a $3 billion investment made by the federal government. The federal government has made similar investments in other projects designed to help Americans cut down on the use of fossil fuels. In 2008 Congress approved a hefty tax break to help homeowners convert their homes to solar energy. The tax break represented 30 percent of the cost of installing solar thermal or photovoltaic systems, which in effect knocked $10,000 or more off the cost of installing the systems. Businesses converting to solar power could also obtain the tax breaks.

Even before Congress approved the tax incentives, the solar industry was taking off. According to the U.S. Department of Energy (DOE), in 1998 just 15,069 photovoltaic solar panels were in use in America. By 2007 that number had grown to 280,475. Among the users of solar power are some of America's largest businesses—Ford Motor Company, PepsiCo, Whole Foods, and Google have all installed solar panels on the roofs of their factories, offices, warehouses, and stores. Even BP Global—an oil company formerly known as British Petroleum—has installed solar panels on the roofs of its gasoline stations to provide electricity for its gas pumps.

Despite the enthusiasm of many individuals and corporations, by 2007 solar systems were providing just one-hundredth of 1 percent of the electricity generated in the United States. Renewable energy advocates concede that it will take a long time for solar power to make a significant dent in fossil fuel use; nevertheless, they urge consumers to recognize the benefits of solar power, including the simple fact that solar power is virtually maintenance free. Individuals and companies that install solar collectors on their roofs can count on decades of electrical production, free of moving parts that often require repairs and maintenance.

Germany: The Unlikely Leader in Solar Energy

Germany is hardly known for its sunny weather. In fact, the people of Portugal enjoy twice as many sunny days a year as the Germans. And yet Germany is by far the world leader in making use of solar energy.

Fifteen of the world's 20 largest photovoltaic farms are located in Germany. Moreover, the country's solar farms generate half the solar-powered electricity in the world. And yet less than one-half of 1 percent of the energy produced in Germany can be attributed to solar power. Even so, the government intends to keep devoting resources to renewable energy, with a goal of increasing solar's share of energy output in Germany to 3 percent by 2020.

Germany also hopes to become the world leader in manufacturing solar panels, which the country exports to other countries. The German solar panel industry grows by about 20 percent per year, and in 2006 German companies manufactured 15 percent of all panels used in the world. Says Carsten Koernig, managing director of the German Solar Industry Association, "It's been very important to create the necessary market in Germany. We not only want to master the German market, but to conquer the world market as well."

Quoted in Craig Whitlock, "Cloudy Germany a Powerhouse in Solar Energy," *Washington Post*, May 5, 2007. www.washingtonpost.com.

At Georgetown University in Washington, D.C., for example, solar panels installed on the roof of the school's Intercultural Center in the 1980s are still producing power. Said renewable energy advocates Jay Inslee, a member of Congress from Washington State, and Bracken Hendricks, a senior fellow at the Washington, D.C.–based think tank Center for American Progress, "We cannot expect all Americans to rush out and put up solar cells, but it is reasonable to believe that in the very near future, a substantial portion of new construction will include solar."[16]

Concerns About Wind Power

The U.S. Congress has also provided tax incentives to help people install their own wind turbines, which can cost $30,000 or more. Even with the tax incentives, which can reduce the cost of erecting the towers by 30 percent, most homeowners encounter many difficulties as they invest in wind power. For starters, the turbines require tall towers. In order to be effective, turbines have to be taller than everything else in the neighborhood—utility poles, trees, buildings—so that the air currents are not impeded before they strike the turbine blades. Therefore, most turbines have to be at least 80 feet (24.4m) tall. In America, city and town governments are hesitant to permit towers of such heights because of safety issues—local officials worry that children will try to climb them or that the blades will fly off. Also, the turbines are often very noisy.

Most of the individuals who have erected their own turbines are farmers or residents of rural areas, but even they have encountered resistance. In the tiny town of Bourne, Massachusetts, Francis and Wendie Holland invested $40,000 in a 132-foot wind turbine (40.2m) they erected on their property. The Hollands never got to use their turbine, though, because the Bourne town council balked at providing a permit for the project, finding it too dangerous and too noisy. Brian Wall, an attorney for the town council, said local officials were particularly concerned that during winter, chunks of ice would form on the blades on windless days and then fly off once the turbines started spinning. "If this 1,600 pound [blade] falls or something falls off it in the area around it—it needs to be safe,"[17] insisted Wall.

Bourne officials did make attempts to work with the Hollands, contending that they would have approved the tower had it been no higher than 75 feet (22.9m). The Hollands insisted, though, that the tower needed to rise higher than that level because of the height of the surrounding terrain. Said Wendie Holland: "It's lu-

"We cannot expect all Americans to rush out and put up solar cells, but it is reasonable to believe that in the very near future, a substantial portion of new construction will include solar."[16]

— Jay Inslee, member of Congress from Washington State, and Bracken Hendricks, senior fellow at the Washington, D.C.–based think tank Center for American Progress.

dicrous. We were trying to make our bills smaller as we got older, in a clean and responsible fashion, and it boggles my mind that ordinary people like us aren't allowed to do that."[18]

While communities wrestle with issues of safety and height restrictions, turbine manufacturers have been developing new designs they hope will put many safety fears to rest. New turbines that are starting to reach the market feature smaller blades that are, nevertheless, still able to produce power with wind speeds as low as 6 miles (9.66km) per hour. Moreover, the turbines can be mounted on chimneys or towers that are no higher than 30 feet (9m)—about the size of a Ham radio tower, which most communities permit. Small turbines are capable of generating about 15 percent of a home's electricity.

In these small turbines the blades spin on a vertical axis, resembling an egg beater, rather than the large, propeller-like blades that are common in larger turbines. Jay Leno, the TV comic who also writes a column for *Popular Mechanics* on technology, installed one on top of his garage. "Even the slightest little breeze spins the . . . blades, cranks the generator and creates power,"[19] says Leno.

Destruction of the Amazon

While wind turbines and solar panels may help cut carbon emissions, it is believed that some attempts to manufacture renewable energy are actually speeding climate change. In Brazil huge tracts of the Amazon rain forest are being cut down to make land available for the country's sugarcane crop. Sugarcane is in great demand as a component of the biofuel ethanol. To enhance the production of a fuel additive that would cut down on carbon emissions, one of the world's most precious natural habitats—the Amazon rain forest—is being sacrificed.

The deforestation of the Amazon and other natural areas actually causes *more* global warming than biofuels are believed to prevent. For starters, jungles are typically deforested by burning down the trees and shrubs, thus releasing carbon into the atmosphere. Also, trees and other vegetation do a very good job of absorbing the heat of the sun—removing large swaths of trees, shrubs, and grasslands means there is less vegetation to absorb the heat, which means the soil and the oceans must do the job of absorbing the

Trees in the Amazon rain forest have been cut down to make way for the planting of sugarcane, which is a key biofuel ingredient. Such destruction may contribute to climate change because it leaves fewer trees to absorb heat and carbon dioxide.

heat. Finally, by deforesting large regions of the planet, the process of photosynthesis breaks down. During photosynthesis, trees absorb carbon dioxide from the air; the carbon dioxide molecule is then broken down by the tree, with the carbon secreted in the plant and its roots, while the oxygen is returned to the air. With fewer trees, more carbon dioxide remains in the air. Experts believe that deforestation accounts for some 20 percent of all carbon pollution on Earth. One study published in the journal *Science* concluded that when deforestation is taken into account, biofuels result in *twice* the carbon emissions of gasoline.

By 2007 the drive to expand the sugarcane crop into the Amazon rain forest had contributed to the loss of a tract of jungle the size of Rhode Island. Some environmentalists fear that eventually the Amazon rain forest will be reduced to a desert. "You can't protect it," says John Carter, a Texan who owns a ranch in the forest. "There's too much money to be made by tearing it down. Out here, on the frontier, you really see the market at work."[20]

Other regions of the planet are facing similar deforestation. In Asia farmers in Indonesia and Malaysia have bulldozed over or burned down thousands of acres of forested land to grow trees that produce palm oil, which can also be refined into ethanol.

Economists cite one final drawback of biofuels: Because farmers can make more money growing plants that are turned into ethanol, they have devoted fewer acres to growing crops for food. That means the ethanol business is, in effect, helping to drive up worldwide food prices, which makes it more difficult to get food to hungry people. A 2004 University of Minnesota study predicted that by 2025, the growth of worldwide agriculture would reduce the number of hungry people on the planet to 625 million. In 2007, in light of the fast-moving expansion of the ethanol industry, the authors of the study felt compelled to revise their conclusions. Now they are predicting that by 2025 there will be 1.2 billion hungry people on the planet.

However, there are alternatives to using food crops to make biofuels. Switchgrass, for example, is a naturally growing grass found mostly on prairie land. Switchgrass grows on land that is not arable for food crops; therefore, farmers can grow switchgrass without taking acreage out of food production. "This is an energy crop that can be grown on marginal land,"[21] says Ken Vogel, a scientist for the U.S. Department of Agriculture. Switchgrass grows mostly in Nebraska, North Dakota, and South Dakota. The DOE is providing $1.2 billion in grants to build six refineries that are designed specifically to convert switchgrass into ethanol. The refineries will also be able to convert forestry waste, such as wood chips and sawdust, into ethanol.

Fossil Fuels Remain Practical

Because solar, wind, and biofuels may not provide immediate benefits, many critics suggest that political leaders would do well to maintain fossil fuels as part of the nation's energy strategy. Says Newt Gingrich:

> Any strategy that does not substantially increase the domestic production of fossil fuels is a strategy for higher prices and growing scarcities. And we certainly have the resources to boost production, since America has the world's largest supply of fossil fuels. We have much more coal than any other country, along with abundant oil and natural gas reserves. The natural resources are there—we just need the government to allow us to extract them.[22]

Gingrich argues that some 10 billion gallons (37.85 billionL) of oil are available in the Arctic National Wildlife Refuge, and by tapping that source Americans can go a long way toward reducing their reliance on foreign oil producers. The refuge is a 19-million-acre region (7.69 million ha) in northern Alaska that is protected under federal law against industrial incursion, including oil drilling.

Meanwhile, many energy experts believe coal can be made to burn cleaner. Under this concept, known as clean coal technology, carbon dioxide is siphoned off as the coal is burned, then compressed into liquid form. The liquid carbon dioxide is transported through pipelines for storage underground or in abandoned oil fields, or even beneath the sea. Several American utilities have launched studies to determine the economic viability of constructing clean coal plants. As with all new technologies, the process promises to be expensive. That is why in 2009 the federal government started making more than $3 billion in grants available to power companies pursuing clean coal projects. "We need to get off the dime with this and build some full-scale projects to demonstrate this technology at scale, but the price tag per project is $800 million to $1 billion,"[23] says Edward S. Rubin, an environmental engineering professor at Carnegie Mellon University in Pittsburgh, Pennsylvania.

Environmentalists generally oppose clean coal technology, insisting that simply removing the carbon from the emissions does not get rid of the carbon, it merely puts it somewhere else. Moreover, they argue that carbon is only one of the pollutants emitted by coal. As the ash spill in Kingston proved, there are many other toxic hazards that can be attributed to coal. Says Michael Brune, executive director of Rainforest Action Network, an environmental group:

> The dirty secret of "'clean coal" is that, after more than twenty years of government and industry research and billions in subsidies, not a single coal plant in the world can be called clean. [They] do not address most other forms of air and water pollution. They do not give millions of Americans living

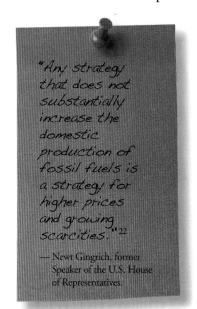

"Any strategy that does not substantially increase the domestic production of fossil fuels is a strategy for higher prices and growing scarcities."[22]

— Newt Gingrich, former Speaker of the U.S. House of Representatives.

Killing Birds with Wind Turbines

Environmentalists have many concerns about wind turbines because they pose a threat to birds that fly into the blades. In fact, environmental groups have been particularly critical of a wind farm that was erected in Altamont, California. The farm includes some 5,400 wind turbines that, since the 1980s, have been responsible for killing 22,000 birds—including 400 golden eagles, which are federally protected birds. Says a publication of the Sierra Club, one of the nation's most influential environmental groups, "Had studies been done before the 5,400-turbine facility was built in the 1980s, they would have shown that the Altamont Pass is an important migration route and wintering area. . . . Better placement of wind farms and individual turbines is key to reducing bird fatalities."

In Altamont, officials are in the process of replacing the bird-killing wind turbines; over the next 10 years, 1 new turbine will replace 15 old ones, producing the same amount of power but making the wind farm far safer for wildlife.

Meanwhile, wind farms in Pennsylvania and West Virginia have been responsible for killing thousands of bats. Environmentalists have endorsed efforts to conduct studies of bird and bat populations and their migratory habits before wind farms are erected to ensure the turbines are not constructed in their paths. Indeed, a study of bird habitats on the south shore of Long Island in New York State helped planners select a location for a wind farm that is likely to have a minimal effect on bird populations.

Francis Cerra Whittelsey, "The Birds and the Breeze," *Sierra*, January/February 2007. www.sierraclub.org.

near coal-fired power plants their basic human right to clean air and safe water. They do not stop mountaintop removal and other unsafe and destructive forms of coal mining, nor do they prevent creation of millions of tons of toxic waste.[24]

Upgrading the Grid

Critics of renewable fuels argue that unlike solar, wind, and other alternative sources, the infrastructure is already in place to deliver oil, coal, and natural gas to customers. Oil and natural gas companies have erected derricks, pumpjacks, and ocean-based drilling platforms in some of the remotest corners of the globe. They also own huge supertankers, some capable of shipping 2 million barrels, or roughly 84 million gallons (318 million L), of crude oil anywhere in the world. Refineries already operate 24 hours a day, 7 days a week, turning crude oil into gasoline, heating oil, and other products. Meanwhile, coal companies are well-entrenched, serving as important components of the economies of many states.

Moreover, thousands of miles of high-voltage utility lines have been laid, linking coal-fired electrical plants and nuclear plants to population and industrial centers. Renewable energy advocates concede that the infrastructure to deliver the electricity from new wind farms that would be erected in the Plains states or solar farms established in the Southwest deserts is missing and that it could take years to develop it. "The current high-voltage transmission grid imposes constraints on the deployment of new renewable energy such as wind, solar, and geothermal power because it simply does not currently go where many of these renewable energy resources will be developed,"[25] says Hendricks.

The cost of connecting these new renewable energy sources to the grid, which is the nationwide interconnection of all electric utilities and their power lines, is believed to be high. According to U.S. Secretary of Energy Steven Chu, it could cost as much as $100 billion to modernize the grid and extend it to the places where new renewable energy resources are likely to be located.

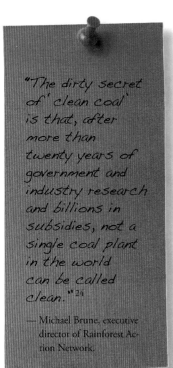

"The dirty secret of 'clean coal' is that, after more than twenty years of government and industry research and billions in subsidies, not a single coal plant in the world can be called clean."[24]

— Michael Brune, executive director of Rainforest Action Network.

Congress has already taken steps to modernize the grid. In 2009 federal lawmakers appropriated $4.5 billion to begin upgrading the grid so that it would be more accessible to renewable energy resources. Hendricks says the action by Congress is an important first step, but making the grid truly accessible to wind, solar, and other renewable energy resources will also take investments by state governments, electric power companies, and consumers, who may find themselves shouldering some of the cost in their monthly electric bills. Said Hendricks, "Constructing a national clean-energy smart grid is the next great challenge, and it will require similar public commitment, a national sense of purpose, and collective sharing of costs in order to realize far greater public benefits."[26]

Certainly, short-term programs like Cash for Clunkers can provide a small measure of relief from fossil fuel use, and other programs, such as the tax credit for installing solar and wind systems, can help homeowners and businesses make long-term commitments to renewable energy. Still, given the problems that families like the Hollands have experienced, as well as the genuine threat

The infrastructure for production and delivery of fossil fuels, including offshore oil rigs, reaches all corners of the globe. A similar infrastructure for renewable fuels does not yet exist and could be years in the making.

of biofuel production to the Amazon rain forest, the widespread practicality of solar, wind, and other renewable resources has yet to be proved, at least at this point. It appears that political leaders, scientists, and others have a lot of information to sort through and decisions to make about the best way to guarantee access to energy while not further damaging the planet.

Facts

- One hour's worth of sunlight that strikes the Earth contains more energy than the entire human population uses in a year.

- In Germany the first clean coal plant became operational in 2008 and will undergo testing until 2011, while in Great Britain a clean coal plant is expected to become operational in 2014.

- Wind turbines provide about 1.3 percent of the electricity generated in the United States, about enough to power 4.6 million homes.

- It would take one person a year to eat all the corn that is used to manufacture enough ethanol to fill a single tank of a large American car.

- During a 6-month period in 2007, 750,000 acres (303,514ha) of Amazon rain forest were converted into cropland for the production of sugarcane used to make ethanol.

- Switchgrass is a perennial crop, meaning it only has to be planted once. Therefore, switchgrass generates 540 percent of the energy used to produce the crop, whereas corn—which has to be replanted every year—produces just 25 percent more energy than the farmers use to cultivate it.

How Affordable Is Renewable Energy?

Trying to determine the cost of replacing fossil fuels with renewable energy sources is an enormously complicated undertaking. Many experts have looked at what it would cost to replace oil, gas, and coal with wind, solar, biomass, and other renewable resources and have been able to provide few solid answers. The reason? Oil, gas, and coal constantly fluctuate in price—they are bought and sold on international markets by speculators who base their bids on a variety of changing factors. Such factors may include the weather forecast for a coming winter season or the status of an oil-producing country's political situation.

If an oil-producing country is at war, it may not be able to continue its exports, which means there would be less oil available on the international market, which means the price for a barrel of crude would rise. Also, the price of oil is largely influenced by the Organization of the Petroleum Exporting Countries, a cartel of the world's largest oil producers that meets periodically to set oil-production quotas as a way of influencing prices. Therefore, it is often solely up to the heads of foreign powers to determine the price of oil.

Sometimes, price fluctuations are quite dramatic. In July 2008 the price of crude oil hit an all-time high of $145 a barrel. A few months later the world's economy was mired in a recession, which prompted individuals and industries to use less oil, causing less demand. As a result, the price of crude started falling. In January 2009, just six months after oil hit its all-time high, the price for a barrel of crude oil fell to below $37 a barrel. Prices for coal and natural gas are also known to fluctuate dramatically.

Still, some experts have tried to estimate the cost of replacing fossil fuels with renewable sources. Black & Veatch, a Kansas company that builds coal-, gas-, and wind-powered electric power plants, calculated how much it costs each energy source to generate a kilowatt-hour of electricity. A kilowatt-hour is the use of 1,000 watts of electricity for an hour. It is the unit used by electric companies to bill their customers. For example, a homeowner who illuminates 16 60-watt lightbulbs over the course of an hour has incurred the cost of 1 kilowatt-hour.

Black & Veatch determined that a kilowatt-hour produced by a coal-fired plant costs 7.8 cents, while a gas-fired plant produces energy at 10.6 cents per kilowatt-hour. Cost of a kilowatt-hour produced by a nuclear plant is 10.8 cents. Finally, the company found, the cost of a kilowatt-hour produced by wind turbines is 12 cents, meaning that it costs nearly 50 percent more to make electricity with wind than it does with coal.

The Electric Power Research Institute, a nonprofit think tank funded by electric utilities, suggests that the higher costs of wind power are mostly due to the construction costs of wind farms as well as the transmission lines needed to connect them to the power grid. Moreover, the institute points out that electric utilities must still keep their coal-fired and nuclear plants running because on days when there is little or no wind, backup sources would have to be tapped to produce electricity. Therefore, the electric utility that spends hundreds of millions of dollars developing a wind farm would still have to keep its coal and nuclear plants running, which means the electric customer has to pay for both. Says Robert L. Bradley Jr. of the Institute for Energy Research, "The cost of generating electricity from wind remains stubbornly uneconomical in an increasingly competitive electricity market."[27]

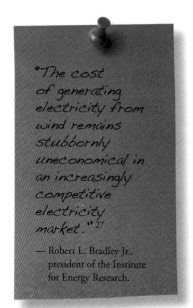

"The cost of generating electricity from wind remains stubbornly uneconomical in an increasingly competitive electricity market."[27]

— Robert L. Bradley Jr., president of the Institute for Energy Research.

The price of gasoline rose precipitously in 2008. In some parts of the United States it reached well over $4 per gallon. But prices for oil and other fossil fuels can fluctuate wildly, making it hard to compare fossil fuel and renewable fuel costs.

The Pickens Plan

The prohibitive cost of establishing wind power as a viable source of energy could be found in the aborted effort by billionaire T. Boone Pickens, who believes a vast wind corridor exists from northern Texas to the Canadian border. Pickens has advocated erecting thousands of wind turbines in the corridor to catch the wind as it sweeps across the American Midwest. "The Department of Energy came out with a study in April of 2007 that said we could generate 20 percent of our electricity from wind," says Pickens. "And the wind power is, you know, clean, it's renewable, it's . . . everything you want. And it's a stable supply of energy."[28]

Pickens made his fortune in the oil business, leasing land in Oklahoma and Texas for oil wells, and so his belief in the promise of wind energy was welcomed by renewable energy advocates, who could rightly claim that even oil businesspeople were now getting the message. Says Carl Pope, executive director of the Sierra Club,

Who Sets the Price of Oil?

Crude oil is traded on the open market, bought and sold by speculators who attempt to gauge worldwide demand for oil, which helps determine the price. If industrialized nations are suffering a recession, demand for oil will drop because manufacturing slows. There is less need for oil used to manufacture plastics and other products, less demand for oil to make gasoline and diesel fuel to transport goods, and less demand by people to buy gasoline for their cars because they have less money and therefore spend less and travel less. As a result, oil prices go down. On the other hand, during a robust economy the price for crude oil usually climbs.

Traders buy and sell "oil contracts" mostly on the New York Mercantile Exchange and the Intercontinental Exchange, which is headquartered in Atlanta, Georgia. Usually, a contract consists of 1,000 barrels of oil. Trading is done both electronically and in person by traders who shout out their orders in "trading pits" located at the exchanges.

The traders buy and sell what are known as futures—they are trading in contracts to deliver oil at a date in the near future, usually three months hence. Therefore, the traders are speculating on what oil will cost three months before the crude is pumped out of the ground. Eventually, the prices paid for the futures contracts make their way to the gasoline pumps, where the cost is passed on to the consumers.

"Mr. Pickens and I probably don't see eye-to-eye on some other matters. But he's right on this one."[29]

In 2008 Pickens proposed the Pickens Plan, a blueprint for reducing America's reliance on fossil fuels, particularly imported oil. The Pickens Plan includes the eventual erection of thousands of wind turbines as well as the establishment of solar farms. To kick off the plan, Pickens announced that he would invest $2 billion to erect 687 wind turbines near Sweetwater, Texas, a community surrounded by vast tracts of windswept prairie land. Pope saw the plan as the beginning of a vast network of solar and wind systems that would work in tandem—on cloudy days the wind turbines would provide energy, while on sunny yet breezeless days the solar panels would do the work. Said Pope, "When it's cloudy in Dallas and the wind is not blowing in Sweetwater, but the sun is blazing in the deserts, solar energy can run all those air conditioners in Dallas. When it's windy in Sweetwater and cloudy in the desert, wind energy from Sweetwater can heat homes in Chicago."[30]

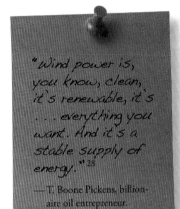

"Wind power is, you know, clean, it's renewable, it's . . . everything you want. And it's a stable supply of energy."[28]

— T. Boone Pickens, billionaire oil entrepreneur.

The initial project was designed to provide as much electricity as a nuclear power plant, but Pickens said he had even grander plans. By 2014 he hoped to quadruple the size of the Sweetwater wind farm, bringing his total investment in wind power up to $8 billion. Under the plan, Pickens hoped to provide electricity to a million homes. Moreover, Pickens said he could envision other entrepreneurs establishing similar wind farms across the Midwest and in other places of the country as well. "There could be lots of Sweetwaters out there,"[31] he said.

But a year after announcing his proposal for the wind farm in Texas, Pickens abruptly withdrew his plans after he was unable to work out an agreement with the state government to extend transmission lines to the wind turbines he proposed to erect. The cost of extending those lines amounted to another $5 billion, bringing the total cost of Pickens's project to some $13 billion. Moreover, the financial incentives to erect the wind turbines fell through when oil and natural gas dropped in price as a result of the 2009 recession. In other words it was cheaper to buy natural gas than the electricity produced by the wind turbines. "It doesn't mean wind is dead," insisted Pickens. "It just means we got a little too quick off the blocks."[32]

Although T. Boone Pickens made his fortune in the oil and gas business, he now advocates development of wind power. However, the worldwide recession of 2008-2009 forced him to postpone his plans for a giant Texas wind farm.

Still, Pickens said he is committed to wind power and intends to buy the initial 687 wind turbines, which should start arriving in 2011. Pickens said he plans to look for other places to establish the wind farm and is considering an alternative site in Texas as well as possible sites in Oklahoma, Wisconsin, and Kansas. "I don't have a garage to put them in, so I've got to start getting ready to use them,"[33] he said.

The Cost of Solar Energy in New Jersey

The failure of even a billionaire to line up financing for a single wind farm illustrates the enormous startup costs involved in replacing fossil fuels with renewable energy sources. Despite those costs, many electricity providers are pushing ahead with projects. In New Jersey, Public Service Electric and Gas Company (PSE&G), a major electric utility that provides power to a number of communities in the state, intends to install solar panels atop some 200,000 utility poles and establish large solar farms throughout its service area. The price tag: $515 million.

To minimize the impact on its customers, PSE&G plans to spread out the cost over a number of years. The New Jersey Division of Rate Counsel, a state agency that monitors electric utility rates, estimated that PSE&G's solar conversion project would add a mere 10 cents per month to the average residential electric bill. "We think it's a good program to get solar started in the state,"[34] said Stefanie Brand, director of the Division of Rate Counsel.

Another tactic PSE&G and other New Jersey power companies intend to employ to help keep the cost down is to locate solar arrays atop buildings rather than on large, open properties. Indeed, New Jersey is home to an abundance of factories, warehouses, and office parks that feature broad and flat roofs—ideal for absorbing sunlight. Moreover, by locating the solar arrays atop buildings, the utilities can cut down on the transmission costs—obviously, expensive power lines do not have to be laid when the customers can be found right below the solar collectors. "One of the things I think will be essential for renewables in the future is that we can demonstrate that they make economic sense being built where there are people to use the electricity,"[35] said Ralph Izzo, chief executive officer of PSE&G.

Nevertheless, Izzo and other experts believe that additional electric rate increases for New Jersey homeowners and business owners are inevitable as the state moves further into renewable energy. State officials said the PSE&G project accounts for just 4 percent of New Jersey's overall plan to make use of renewable resources. Obviously, then, as more and more renewables—other solar projects, wind farms, biomass projects, and geothermal plants—are added into the state's inventory of power producers, the homeowners and business owners who pay electric bills are likely to see additional increases. According to Izzo, the challenge for government officials as well as electric utility executives will be in convincing homeowners that converting to renewable resources may be expensive, but the cost of climate change might be greater. Said Izzo: "We've got to stop pretending solar power will lower the cost of energy. It's going to increase the cost, and people have got to understand why it's worth more."[36]

"We've got to stop pretending solar power will lower the cost of energy. It's going to increase the cost, and people have got to understand why it's worth more."[36]

— Ralph Izzo, chief executive officer of Public Service Electric and Gas Company of New Jersey.

Aid for Homeowners

Just as large utilities must shoulder enormous costs when converting to renewable energy, homeowners and business owners who want to install their own rooftop solar systems or replace their furnaces with geothermal heat pumps find that the costs are steep as well. Indeed, the cost of converting the typical single-family home to solar power often runs between $25,000 and $50,000. In return, the homeowner's electric bill may be sliced by as much as 75 percent, but even so, it could take many years before the homeowner would see the savings pay for the cost of installation. Home-based geothermal systems are less expensive—the typical system costs less than $30,000. Still, it is estimated that it would take many years before the energy savings pay for the cost of installation.

To help homeowners pay for the cost of converting to renewable energy, Congress has approved the tax break that equates to 30 percent of the cost of the system. State governments have also enacted programs to help homeowners and business owners convert to renewable energy sources. Starting in 2009, for example, Pennsylvania has provided homeowners with grants to help them convert their homes to solar energy—the grants pay for up to 35 percent of the cost for the conversions. This means that when the federal and state programs are combined, homeowners in Pennsylvania can receive government help covering up to 65 percent of the cost of converting their homes to solar energy. Therefore, to a Pennsylvania homeowner a $50,000 photovoltaic system really costs just $17,500. When the grants and tax breaks are factored into the cost of converting the home, the payback period could be slashed to 10 years or less.

Soon after they retired, Titus and Trude Miller installed a photovoltaic system on the roof of their home in Windsor Township, Pennsylvania. The system cost $26,000, but the Millers received aid totaling $16,900 in federal tax incentives and the state grant. Therefore, the out-of-pocket cost to the Millers was less than $10,000. "Putting a solar system in sounds like it's

> "Putting a solar system in sounds like it's terribly expensive, but with all the incentives for people who are able to use the state and federal programs, there is actually a payback in about seven years."[37]
>
> — Titus Miller, resident of Windsor Township, Pennsylvania.

terribly expensive, but with all the incentives for people who are able to use the state and federal programs, there is actually a payback in about seven years," said Titus Miller. "Think about buying a car for $26,000 that depreciates 25 percent as soon as you drive it out of the shop, but this thing keeps generating and generating."[37]

Another factor that makes the projects financially attractive is that in certain months, the owners of alternative energy systems can actually make more electric power than they use. Typically, this happens in the spring and the fall, when electric heaters and air conditioners are not often in use. Under these circumstances, the power companies are required by law to buy the electricity from the owners of the renewable systems. Usually, the utilities provide a credit on the next month's bill.

And still another incentive provides the owners of renewable systems such as photovoltaic arrays and wind turbines renewable energy credits that can be sold on the open market to utilities. Many states have adopted laws requiring utilities to manufacture some of their energy through renewable methods. To help achieve their goals, utilities can claim the power generated by systems installed in homes or businesses. To claim the power, they must buy the rights from the owners. Most owners of small home-based systems sell their credits to so-called aggregators, who put together blocks of credits and in turn sell them to utilities. Most homeowners find they can earn between $1,500 and $2,000 a year by selling their energy credits to aggregators.

Green Mortgages

By installing renewable energy systems in their houses, homeowners find their monthly electric, gas, and home-heating-oil bills are cheaper, sometimes by hundreds of dollars. Those types of savings can even make it possible for many prospective homeowners to buy their first houses or trade up to larger houses.

To buy a home most people must first obtain a mortgage. This is a loan made by banks or similar financial institutions, sometimes for hundreds of thousands of dollars, that enables people to afford their homes. Most mortgages are for very long terms,

The 10 Solar Friendly States

According to the Seattle, Washington–based environmental group Cooler Planet, 10 states provide homeowners with at least 35 percent of the cost of installing solar energy systems through a combination of the 30 percent federal tax credit as well as state-financed rebates, grants, or low-interest loans. Those states include New Mexico, Colorado, Pennsylvania, Maryland, Massachusetts, Connecticut, New Jersey, California, Oregon, and Minnesota.

Colorado provides the most aid—homeowners can receive financial assistance totaling as much as 85 percent of the cost to install solar systems, which can typically cost some $50,000. Most of the other states on the list provide about 50 percent of the cost. Oregon and Maryland provide the least aid, offering homeowners assistance that totals 35 percent to install solar thermal or photovoltaic systems.

Oregon has the longest record of providing assistance to homeowners—according to Cooler Planet, Oregon first offered state tax incentives to individuals to install solar systems in the 1970s.

Cooler Planet pointed out that the value of the solar systems depends largely on the number of sunny days a year. Therefore, people who live in the sunniest states get more value for their money. Among the states on the list, Cooler Planet pointed out that New Mexicans get the most value for their money—their state typically experiences 320 to 340 sunny days a year, while in Colorado, the sun typically shines between 300 and 320 days a year. Of the states on the list, Minnesota experiences the fewest sunny days a year—Minnesotans typically see between 180 and 220 sunny days a year.

usually 30 years. Since the loans are designed to be paid back over 30 years, the payments are typically several hundred dollars to a few thousand dollars a month.

Still, some people barely qualify for their mortgages. Often, people who are on the edge are young couples with little money to use as a down payment on the property. This means a young couple would have to borrow more money to be able to afford a home. When loan officers from banks determine a couple's ability to repay the mortgage, they look at the monthly income earned by the husband and wife as well as their other obligations, usually the money they are repaying on other loans. (Typically, people also find themselves paying off credit card debt, student loans, and car loans.) Many mortgage officers will turn down prospective buyers if they already have too much debt. In deciding whether buyers can afford the monthly mortgage payments, loan officers also take into account projected utility costs. These costs impact how much money the buyers are likely to have available to them each month. Banks have recognized the utility savings that renewable energy systems often provide to homeowners, sometimes amounting to a few hundred dollars a month. This has led to a special class of mortgages available to people who buy homes equipped with solar, wind, or geothermal systems. These loans are known as energy efficient mortgages or green mortgages. In many cases couples who qualify for green mortgages will be approved for the loans even if they have a lot of credit card debt as well as student loans and car loans to pay off.

Mortgage lenders are also willing to lend money to people who buy homes equipped with renewable energy systems because they know that utility rates are likely to keep rising, and therefore people whose energy bills remain low are not likely to be driven out of their homes by spiraling costs for oil, gas, or electricity. Peter Milewski is director of the mortgage insurance division for MassHousing, a state-supported financing agency in Massachusetts that lends mortgage money to low- and middle-income buyers. He says: "As energy costs increase, homes that have energy

> " The big, concentrated, renewable-energy projects are necessary. Just putting solar panels on buildings is not enough."[39]
>
> — Anthony Brunello, deputy secretary for energy in the California Natural Resources Agency.

efficiency are going to be better for the home buyer in terms of financial stability. . . . Anything that can reduce and stabilize the cost of energy in this volatile energy environment is a good thing for us to be involved in."[38]

Fossil Fuel Costs Rise

Homeowners and business owners are not the only energy consumers who have received government aid for solar, wind, and geothermal projects. In 2009, $8 billion was made available by the federal government to state and local governments to help them finance large-scale renewable energy projects, such as developing photovoltaic and wind systems to power college dormitories and other university buildings as well as hospitals, government buildings, and similar public facilities. "The big, concentrated, renewable-energy projects are necessary," says Anthony Brunello, deputy secretary for energy in the California Natural Resources Agency. "Just putting solar panels on buildings is not enough."[39]

Indeed, it may cost a lot of money to build a wind farm or a solar farm. Those costs are always passed on to the consumers in the form of higher energy bills. Even homeowners who seek to slash their energy bills by installing their own geothermal heat pumps or rooftop solar arrays face bills totaling many thousands of dollars, and therefore it is often years before they start receiving the economic benefits of renewable energy.

In the meantime the cost of fossil fuels hardly remains stable. While it may be true that the cost of oil, natural gas, and coal may rise and fall in price, sometimes in very short periods of time, over the long term fossil fuel prices almost always go up. Thirty years ago gasoline cost about $1 a gallon at the pump; in recent years it has climbed higher than $4 a gallon. Anybody who questions whether fossil fuels will continue to rise in price need only ask Pickens, who has spent nearly 60 years in the oil business. "We are very close to a disaster for the country," Pickens contends. "[Oil] is expensive now, it's going to get more expensive."[40] It may cost a lot of money to install the infrastructure to take advantage of nature's renewable energy sources but the cost of sunshine and wind and other such resources never goes up in price.

Facts

- California has committed $3.3 billion in grants to home-owners to convert their homes to solar energy; the state's goal by the year 2019 is for a million homeowners to install photovoltaic systems.

- Investment in renewable energy sources slowed in 2008 and 2009 after natural gas dropped in price by 72 percent due to the discovery of new gas reserves as well as a decrease in demand caused by the worldwide recession.

- California real estate experts have estimated that every $1,000 a year that is cut from a home's energy bills adds $15,000 to the resale value of the home.

- According to a report in the *New York Times*, some experts have calculated that it costs 50 percent more to generate electricity through wind than it does through coal.

- The conversion to renewable energy is likely to cost tens of billions of dollars, but oil also represents a large expense for business and consumers. The United States imports 70 percent of its oil, which costs consumers some $700 billion a year.

- MassHousing has found that saving $50 a month in energy costs can enable people to qualify for up to $15,000 more in mortgage money to help them buy their homes.

What Policies Should Guide Renewable Energy's Future?

Lake County, California, is located just north of San Francisco. The county takes its name from Clear Lake, a 44,000-acre body of water (17,806ha) that is the largest and oldest lake in California. Scientific tests have indicated that Clear Lake may be some 500,000 years old.

Sitting below Clear Lake is a series of volcanoes. Volcanoes are located atop tremendous reservoirs of geothermal energy—that is why their eruptions spew tons of hot ash into the air while molten lava streams down their mountainsides. Near Clear Lake, Cobb Mountain and Mount Conocoti are both volcanoes. None of the Lake County volcanoes are likely to erupt—all are dormant, meaning massive amounts of rock beneath the volcanoes have shifted over time, covering up the hot spots that generate volcanic activity.

Nevertheless, it is the huge potential of the geothermal energy below Clear Lake and elsewhere throughout Lake County that has drawn power companies to the region, where they have established the country's largest geothermal field. Deep beneath the surface of the ground, the heat has been measured at 450°F (232°C). To bring that heat to the surface, power companies pump water into the earth, where it comes into contact with the heat and makes steam. "All we're doing here is mining heat," says Louis Capuano Jr., chief executive officer of Thermasource, a geothermal exploration company. "We're pulling heat out of the ground. The water is just a medium that carries heat back to the surface."[41]

The Potential of Geothermal Energy

By 2010 California officials hope to generate 20 percent of the state's power through renewable resources, with half coming from geothermal energy. In fact, geothermal energy is regarded as having far more potential to meet energy needs than either wind or solar. Unlike wind, geothermal energy continues to produce power on days when there is no breeze, and unlike solar, geothermal continues to be reliable on cloudy days and at night as well. "Wind and solar are great resources, but they are intermittent by their nature, which means you've got to keep a lot of backup power on line. Right now, that [backup power] is oil and gas,"[42] says Tom King, an executive of U.S. Renewables, which invests in geothermal exploration.

Already, some 800,000 homes in northern California are powered by the geothermal energy found 8,000 feet (2,438m) beneath the soil of Lake County. It is that type of potential that led the federal government in 2009 to commit $338 million to help fund geothermal exploration projects throughout the United States. Soon, some 100 projects searching for geothermal energy were underway in 13 states. "Geothermal energy is hot . . . right now,"[43] says Karl Gawell, director of the trade group Geothermal Energy Association.

"In Kyoto, our mission was to persuade other nations to find common ground so we could make realistic and achievable commitments to reduce greenhouse gas emissions."[50]

— Bill Clinton, forty-second president of the United States.

Federal Government Involvement in Renewable Energy

The federal government's interest in developing renewable energy sources dates back to the 1970s, when energy security first surfaced as an issue for many Americans. President Jimmy Carter, who took office in 1977, urged Americans to conserve energy— he would often address Americans on national TV while wearing a sweater, showing that he preferred to put on an extra layer of clothing rather than turn up the thermostat in the White House.

Several volcanoes lie beneath Clear Lake (pictured) in northern California. Though the volcanoes are dormant, experts believe they offer huge potential for geothermal energy. Many power companies have come to the region to explore that possibility.

Carter also ordered solar thermal collectors installed on the roof of the White House and established the Solar Energy Research Institute, a federal agency charged with exploring new technologies to make use of the sun's energy. To run the agency, Carter appointed Dennis Hayes, an attorney and engineer and the founder of Earth Day.

The Carter presidency was short-lived—Carter lost his reelection bid in 1980. The new president, Ronald Reagan, soon ordered the Solar Energy Research Institute stripped of most of its funding. Recalls Hayes, "In June or July of 1981, on the bleakest day of my professional life, they descended on the Solar Energy Research Institute, fired about half of our staff and all of our contractors, including two people who went on to win Nobel prizes in other fields, and reduced our $130 million budget by $100 million."[44]

Reagan had been elected on a promise to reduce the size of government, eliminating all but the most vital federal programs.

Clearly, Reagan did not regard renewable energy as a program vital to the national interest. He even ordered the solar collectors taken off the roof of the White House. (The panels were not scrapped; they were eventually acquired by Unity College in Maine and installed on the roof of the school's cafeteria.)

Hayes soon left the Solar Energy Research Institute, but the agency has managed to remain a part of the federal government. It was eventually transferred to the U.S. Department of Energy (DOE) and renamed the National Renewable Energy Laboratory. Also, its funding was restored: Congress provides the laboratory with operating budgets of about $328 million a year.

Experimenting with Silicon

The National Renewable Energy Laboratory, headquartered in Golden, Colorado, serves as a research and development arm of the DOE, exploring ways in which renewable energy resources can be refined and made more available to American homes and businesses. A large part of the laboratory's job is to experiment with the materials and technologies used in renewable resources to see whether those sources can be made cheaper and more efficient.

For example, in recent years the laboratory has focused on reducing the cost of photovoltaic (PV) cells. Most PV cells are coated with a layer of crystalline silicon, the substance that acts as the "conductor," transferring the sun's energy into electricity. To make the collectors more affordable, the laboratory has explored substituting a similar substance, amorphous silicon.

Silicon is a common element. As the terms suggest, crystalline silicon is found in crystal form, while amorphous silicon can be laid down as a film. (Desktop calculators powered by light employ amorphous silicon in their solar cells.) Crystalline silicon is a much more effective substance for PV cells—it is twice as efficient as amorphous silicon in turning sunlight into energy. However, amorphous silicon may still have widespread potential to create solar energy because it takes 100 times less amorphous silicon to create the same amount of energy produced by crystalline silicon. PV cells made with amorphous silicon are known as thin film cells. Currently, about 40 percent of the cost of a PV cell is devoted to the silicon. Obviously, if less silicon can be used in the cell, the cell

A technician checks a component of a photovoltaic cell as it rolls off the assembly line. The type of silicon traditionally used to make such cells is costly but other, less expensive forms of silicon are being tested.

would be cheaper. Says John Benner, manager of a division of the laboratory called the National Center for Photovoltaics, "If you're making a thin-film module, much of that cost will go away."[45]

The Waxman-Markey Bill

The government influences energy policy in more ways than just making grant money available for new energy systems or exploring which types of silicon work best in PV cells. Over the years Congress has passed many laws affecting how Americans use energy. For example, in 1978 Congress mandated that car manufacturers had to improve the fuel efficiencies of their cars—these mandates became known as the Corporate Average Fuel Economy, or CAFE, standards. Back in 1978 the CAFE standard for passenger cars was 18 miles per gallon (7.65km/L) in city driving; by 2010 that standard had risen to 27 miles per gallon (11.48km/L). Moreover, in 2007 Congress passed the Energy Independence and Security Act, which further increased the CAFE standards. By 2020 the CAFE standard for a passenger car will be 35 miles per gallon (14.88km/L). The 2007 law took other steps as well, mandating further development of biofuels, providing tax incentives for manufacturers to develop electric cars, and prohibiting sales of incandescent lightbulbs by 2014.

By late 2009 even more sweeping energy legislation was under consideration. Lawmakers debated the proposed Waxman-Markey American Clean Energy and Security Act. (The bill is named for its authors, U.S. Representatives Henry Waxman of California and Edward J. Markey of Massachusetts.) The main provision of Waxman-Markey is the establishment of a so-called cap-and-trade system. Under cap and trade, large industrial polluters are permitted to buy credits, also known as offsets, to emit carbon from their smokestacks. The sellers of the offsets are industries that have found ways to cap emissions. It is believed that a robust market in the carbon credits will emerge, prompting many large companies to cut their carbon emissions dramatically so that they will be able to earn substantial profits by selling the offsets to polluters who cannot find ways to scale back on carbon emissions. The goal of Waxman-Markey is to cut carbon emissions to a level that is 4 percent lower than the level of emissions produced in 1990.

> "Kyoto would have wrecked our economy. I couldn't in good faith have signed Kyoto."[51]
>
> — George W. Bush, forty-third president of the United States.

Waxman-Markey also includes a requirement that by 2020, electric utilities must generate at least 15 percent of their power from renewable resources. This goal has been heavily criticized by environmental groups and other opponents, who contend that the bill does not go far enough to require electric companies to convert to solar, wind, biomass, and geothermal sources. In fact, when the bill was introduced in early 2009, it set the goal for renewable energy at 25 percent by 2025, but that goal was scaled back after members of Congress from southeastern states applied some intense pressure on the bill's chief sponsors. These Congress members worried that utility companies in their home states would have trouble meeting the goal. Most of those electric companies rely on coal-fired plants, largely because coal is widely available in the Southeast. Thus far, few electric companies in the Southeast have made commitments to renewable sources.

Fair Compromise

Critics of Waxman-Markey such as U.S. Representative Dennis Kucinich of Ohio complained that the bill made too many concessions, particularly the provision that cut back the renewable energy goal from 25 percent to 15 percent. Kucinich pointed out that most electric companies are well on their way to meeting a 15 percent goal anyway, and therefore such a goal would be attained even without the bill.

As such, Kucinich said, the bill fails to use the power of the federal government to force electric companies into taking significant steps toward using renewable resources. "The renewable electricity standard is not an improvement," Kucinich insisted. "The 15 percent renewable energy standard would be achieved even if we failed to act . . . not only can we do better; we have no choice but to do better. Indeed, if we pass a bill that only creates the illusion of addressing the problem, we walk away with only an illusion. The price for that illusion is the opportunity to take substantive action."[46]

Environmental groups were not happy with the bill, either. Damon Moglen, director of the Global Warming Campaign for Greenpeace, said his group opposes Waxman-Markey specifically because the renewable energy goal was cut back to 15 percent. Said Moglen:

> The first piece of legislation attempting to seriously address global warming was introduced in Congress. The bill—authored and introduced by Representatives Waxman and Markey—started off as a good first step toward solving the climate crisis. But following pressure from an all-out . . . lobbying push by the coal, gas and oil industries, the bill looks very different today. . . . Unfortunately, we simply can't support this bill in its current state.[47]

Incandescent Versus Fluorescent

The incandescent bulb has changed little since Thomas Edison figured out how to make one light up in 1879. Essentially, the lightbulb works as electricity passes through a tungsten filament housed inside the glass bulb. The electricity makes the filament very hot, which causes it to glow or "incandesce."

However, incandescent bulbs waste a lot of energy. Anybody who has tried to unscrew a lightbulb just after the switch is turned off knows the bulb is still very hot. All that heat fulfills no purpose—it is essentially wasted energy. Compact fluorescent bulbs work on a different principle. The bulbs contain mercury vapor, which is a gas. When the power is turned on, the electricity prompts the electrons in the mercury atoms to move about quickly and hit the inside walls of the bulb, which are coated with metal compounds known as phosphors. The collision of electrons against the coated walls result in visible light. A compact fluorescent bulb produces less heat and is therefore more efficient than an incandescent bulb.

In 2007 Congress adopted new efficiency standards for lightbulbs that will take effect by 2014. The standards, which require lightbulbs to use at least 25 percent less energy, are too stiff to be met by most incandescent bulbs, meaning that by 2014 most buildings in America will be illuminated with fluorescent lighting.

Waxman defended the legislation, contending that the issue of climate change had been ignored for many years and that many lawmakers who represent coal-producing states were of a mind to continue ignoring the issue. Waxman insisted that convincing those lawmakers to agree to even a modest 15 percent reduction in fossil fuel use represented a fair compromise.

Indeed, as part of the compromise, Waxman said he convinced the coal region lawmakers to agree to a 15 percent cut by 2020—five years earlier than the original bill would have required the larger cut of 25 percent. Moreover, Waxman said, the revised legislation also includes establishment of a national Energy Efficiency Resource Standard (EERS). Currently, a handful of state governments have established such standards, which require electric utilities to obtain a certain amount of capacity from renewable energy resources, even if they do not make it themselves. Among the states that have established EERS programs are California, Connecticut, Hawaii, Nevada, Texas, and Vermont. Some European countries, including Belgium, Great Britain, France, and Italy, have also established EERS-like programs.

"If things go business as usual, we will not live."[52]

— Mohamed Nasheed, president of the Maldives.

Typically, utilities that have trouble meeting their EERS targets can achieve their goals by buying the power generated by wind and solar sources from utilities that have excess renewable resources. As part of the compromise with the coal region lawmakers, Waxman said, he convinced them to agree to a national EERS program, meaning all electrical producers in the United States would have to find ways to obtain renewable energy on the open market. Establishing a national EERS program is expected to cut the nation's reliance on fossil fuels by another 5 percent by 2020. Therefore, Waxman said, the original goal of cutting fossil fuel use by 25 percent by 2025 may not be realized; nevertheless, fossil fuel use will be cut by 20 percent by 2020.

"We worked hard to craft compromises that addressed the legitimate concerns of industry without undermining the integrity of the legislation," Waxman said. "Tackling hard issues that have been ignored for years is never easy."[48] Added Representative Bart Gordon of Tennessee, who pushed hard for the 15 percent renewables goal, "I think we have put together something pretty good."[49]

Striving for International Cooperation

One of the major requirements of any national energy policy is that it has to be coordinated with energy policies in every other country on the planet. In other words, cutting down on carbon emissions in one country does little good if other countries do not also accept responsibility and enact similar plans. After all, everyone shares the same atmosphere.

In a world in which political leaders often find little common ground on such issues as trade, arms, religious zealotry, and territorial disputes, most world leaders are remarkably in agreement on cutting back on carbon emissions. In fact, in 1997 nearly 200 countries agreed to the terms of an international climate change treaty known as the Kyoto Protocol, named for the city in Japan where the pact was negotiated. The main provisions of Kyoto required the signatories to reduce their carbon emissions to a level at least 5 percent below 1990 levels. By 2005 the legislative bodies of virtually every country on Earth had ratified the Kyoto Protocol. However, one major polluter refused to sign the protocol or abide by its provisions: the United States.

At first American leaders were enthusiastic about the Kyoto terms. Vice President Al Gore was dispatched to Japan to help negotiate the terms of the protocol. At the conclusion of the talks, President Bill Clinton said he welcomed the challenge of meeting the treaty's carbon emission goals. "No nation is more committed to this effort than the United States," Clinton said at the time. "In Kyoto, our mission was to persuade other nations to find common ground so we could make realistic and achievable commitments to reduce greenhouse gas emissions."[50]

Under U.S. law, all international treaties must be ratified by the Senate. Clinton balked at submitting the treaty to the Senate, though, finding that its terms would force American industries to cut back production in order to meet the emissions goals. He feared that such cuts in production would force massive layoffs of American workers, throwing the country into a recession. In 2001, shortly after President George W. Bush took office, he also decided not to submit the Kyoto treaty to the Senate, citing the same reasons as Clinton. "Kyoto would have wrecked our economy," Bush said. "I couldn't in good faith have signed Kyoto."[51]

Moreover, Kyoto also includes a cap-and-trade system that critics believe provides few positive results because major polluters have been given too much leeway to continue polluting, which has failed to spur a market for the offsets. One of the problems found in most international efforts to stem carbon emissions is the desire of developing countries, including China and India, to continue burning fossil fuels to spur industrial growth. Indeed, China and India are believed to account for a quarter of all carbon emissions in the world. Without the participation of the United States, and with developing countries such as China and India permitted to continue their growth by relying on fossil fuels, the goals of the Kyoto Protocol have been largely unmet.

Climate Talks Move to Copenhagen

By 2009 world leaders had recognized the failures of the Kyoto Protocol to stem greenhouse gas emissions and vowed to try again. In December 2009 the United Nations convened a conference on climate change in Copenhagen, Denmark, specifically aimed at making the type of progress on greenhouse gas emissions that eluded the signers of the Kyoto Protocol more than a decade earlier. Representatives from 193 countries participated in the talks. Those who attended the Copenhagen conference said they realized that climate change represented a much more dire emergency than had been recognized at Kyoto. Prior to the conference Mohamed Nasheed, the president of the Maldives, an island nation in the Indian Ocean, said he feared coastal flooding caused by climate change could soon result in the destruction of his country. "If things go business as usual, we will not live,"[52] Nasheed said.

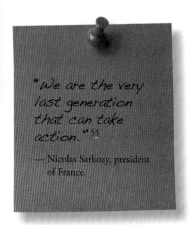

"We are the very last generation that can take action."[55]

—Nicolas Sarkozy, president of France.

This time the United States, as well as other major polluters, signaled more of a commitment to making substantial cuts in carbon emissions. Shortly before the conference convened, U.S. president Barack Obama said, "The developed nations that caused much of the damage to our climate over the last century have a responsibility to lead."[53] Two months before the conference, something of a breakthrough was announced when, in advance of the treaty, representatives from India and China signed a pact committing their countries to developing renewable energy programs. Said Michael Mason, director of conservation at the Grantham Research Institute on Climate Change at the London School of Economics, "When India and China take the lead, the rest usually follow."[54]

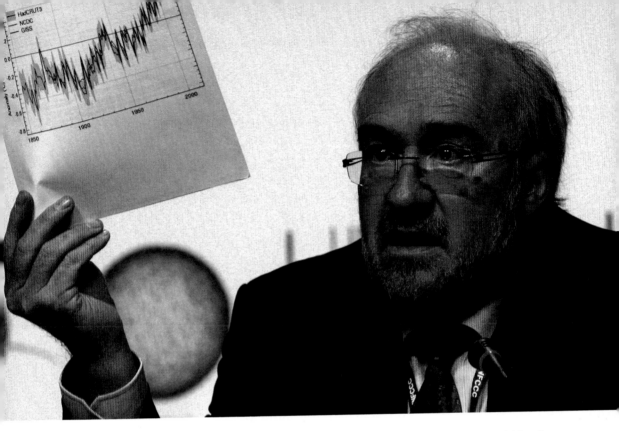

The final agreement, which was negotiated by five of the planet's biggest polluters—the United States, China, India, South Africa, and Brazil—requires industrialized nations to set targets for reducing greenhouse gases with the goal of ensuring the Earth's temperature rises no more than another 3.6°F (2°C). In addition, the industrialized countries said they would raise $100 billion a year through 2020 to help developing countries create industries and jobs without using fossil fuels.

Many of the participants said they recognized that a failure to develop a global strategy to reduce greenhouse gases this time would likely imperil future residents of the planet, subjecting them to severe storms, droughts, species loss, floods, and other forms of devastation. Indeed, each year that greenhouse gas emissions are not scaled back, the industrialized countries of the planet pump 33 billion tons (29.9 million metric tons) of carbon dioxide into the atmosphere. A few weeks before the conference was set to convene, French president Nicolas Sarkozy said, "We are the very last generation that can take action."[55]

World leaders met in Copenhagen, Denmark, in December 2009 for the UN Climate Conference. During the conference the secretary-general of the World Meteorological Organization discusses a temperature chart showing rising world temperatures.

Al Gore's Mission

Al Gore served as vice president from 1993 through 2001. In 2000 he lost the disputed election for president to George W. Bush. Since leaving office Gore has become a major advocate for reducing greenhouse gas emissions. His 2006 book, *An Inconvenient Truth*, is a best seller that critics believe helped convince Americans that the greenhouse effect has been caused by carbon emissions. Wrote Michiko Kakutani, the book critic for the *New York Times*:

> Mr. Gore methodically lays out the probable consequences of rising temperatures: powerful and more destructive hurricanes fueled by warmer ocean waters . . . increased soil moisture evaporation, which means drier land, less productive agriculture and more fires; and melting ice sheets in Antarctica and Greenland, which would lead to rising ocean levels, which in turn would endanger low-lying regions of the world from southern Florida to large portions of the Netherlands.

Gore's efforts have been recognized. In 2006 a film documentary based on the book, also titled *An Inconvenient Truth*, won the Academy Award for Best Documentary. A year later Gore shared the Nobel Peace Prize with the Intergovernmental Panel on Climate Change, a scientific group formed by the United Nations and World Meteorological Organization. Said the Nobel selection committee's citation: "His strong commitment, reflected in political activity, lectures, films and books, has strengthened the struggle against climate change. He is probably the single individual who has done most to create greater worldwide understanding of the measures that need to be adopted."

Michiko Kakutani, "On Global Warming, Passionate Warnings with Pictures," *New York Times*, May 23, 2006, p. E-6.

Quoted in MSNBC, "Gore, U.N. Climate Panel Win Nobel Peace Prize," October 12, 2007. www.msnbc.msn.com.

Facts

- Solar panels were reinstalled on the White House roof in 2003 by order of President George W. Bush. The panels include photovoltaic collectors as well as solar thermal cells, some of which are used to help heat the White House swimming pool.

- Before solar energy research was all but killed by the Reagan administration in 1981, officials of the Solar Energy Research Institute were aiming to convert 25 percent of the power generated in the United States to solar energy by 2000.

- In advance of the UN Climate Change Conference in Copenhagen, Denmark, in December 2009, China made a commitment to derive 15 percent of its energy needs from renewable sources by 2020.

- Although India has made a commitment to develop renewable energy resources, lawmakers in India have steadfastly refused to mandate caps on industries that generate greenhouse gases.

- In addition to California, other states that have invested in developing geothermal resources include Hawaii, Idaho, Alaska, Utah, and Nevada. Internationally, major geothermal producers include Iceland, New Zealand, Indonesia, and the Philippines.

Can People Live Without Fossil Fuels?

For a year Colin Beavan and his family lived carbon neutral—they were determined not to emit any carbon into the atmosphere or otherwise provide waste in any form that could not be recycled and used elsewhere. To achieve their goals, Beavan, along with his wife, Michelle, and their young daughter, Isabella, made dramatic changes in their lifestyles. Living in a ninth-floor apartment in New York City, the Beavans refused to use the elevator, rode bicycles to work, and used only reusable cloth tote bags to carry groceries. When Colin visited a Starbucks coffee shop, he asked the store clerks to pour the coffee into a reusable mug that he provided so that he would not have to throw away a paper cup after consuming the beverage. Soon, the Beavans gave up coffee altogether when they realized that the coffee crop is imported from South America and therefore transported thousands of miles—which means shippers and truckers burn fossil fuels in order to make coffee available to New Yorkers.

Meanwhile, the Beavans replaced the incandescent bulbs in their apartment with compact fluorescent bulbs—but then realized that electricity is made by coal-fired plants, so they decided to turn off the electricity in their apartment and live without it. Instead of turning on the lights, they burned candles. Instead of using a refrigerator, the Beavans kept their food cold with ice. Says Colin:

Michelle says that having no electricity in the apartment is like a nonstop vacation. Every summer night we search for things to do outside—play in the fountain with Isabella's friends in Washington Square Park, make a trip to the river. Then we come home in the dark, put Isabella to bed, and sit up, talking in quiet tones by candlelight.

We go, one night, to the community garden with a jar because fireflies are in season. We catch the tiny lightning flashes, Isabella stares at them through the glass of the jar, we let them go. "Daddy, this is so much fun," she tells me.[56]

After the Beavan family lived for a year without producing carbon, Colin Beavan wrote a book about the experience. The book, titled *No Impact Man*, was published in 2009 to favorable reviews. Critics found a lot of humor in the book, but they also regarded the Beavans' story as an admonishment to people who are giving little thought to the environmental consequences of burning fossil fuels. Indeed, many go about their lives in blissful ignorance—leaving electric lights burning when they are not in the room, leaving the car idling outside while they run into the convenience store, buying imported goods when locally produced goods are readily available. "Beavan's project . . . has significant emotional and ecological heft," wrote Sandy Bauers, the environmental beat reporter for the *Philadelphia Inquirer*. "*No Impact Man* works, most of all, because Beavan is intelligent, funny, provocative and, above all, honest. . . . Beavan's many heartfelt ruminations elevate the book from merely interesting to something profound."[57]

"There's so much you can do to stop bleeding wasted energy. If a house still has single-pane windows, for example, it's almost like having a hole in the wall."[58]

— John Steelman, director of the climate program at the Natural Resources Defense Council.

Cutting Carbon at Home

Most people would probably not take the extraordinary steps that the Beavans took to reduce their reliance on fossil fuels, but there are many steps people can take to eliminate some portions of oil, coal, and natural gas from their lives. One way people can cut down on fossil fuel use is to make their homes more energy efficient. People can look for places in their homes where air from the outside is leaking in. These holes can be patched, and exterior walls can be insulated against the cold outside air. Modern windows can be installed—most are now double paned, meaning each window features an insulating zone of air or gas sandwiched by two panes of glass. With a single-pane window, the temperature on the outside causes the window pane to turn cold, which transfers the chill into the room and makes the heater inside work harder. "There's so much you can do to stop bleeding wasted energy," says John Steelman, director of the climate program at the Natural Resources Defense Council. "If a house still has single-pane windows, for example, it's almost like having a hole in the wall."[58]

Saving energy can also be as simple as adjusting a switch. According to the organization Stop Global Warming, just turning the thermostat in the home down by two degrees in the winter and up by two degrees in the summer can reduce carbon emissions by some 2,000 pounds (907kg) a year. Conservation groups also ask people to unplug their chargers if they are not in use. Many people keep them plugged in even if they are not charging cell phones, MP3 players, and similar devices. However, by keeping them plugged in, the chargers keep drawing power even when they are not doing work.

Many power companies offer free energy audits to their customers. In an energy audit an expert in energy use will examine the home, looking for places where air may be leaking, cell phone chargers may be drawing current, or thermostats may be set too high. Another service that many utilities are making available to their customers is "green tag" options. By paying a little more each month, homeowners can be assured that all their energy is being provided by renewable resources. In Oregon, homeowners pay about $24 more a month for this service. "When you offset your usage through a green tag purchase, you're preventing about 1,400 pounds of carbon dioxide and other greenhouse gas emissions a month, or about 16,800 pounds a year,"[59] says Tom Starrs, a spokesperson for the Bonneville Environmental Foundation in Portland, Oregon.

Wal-Mart Goes Solar

On a wider scale many large and small corporations are investing in renewable energy. In America the huge retail chain Wal-Mart

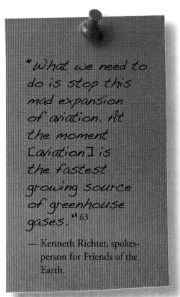

"What we need to do is stop this mad expansion of aviation. At the moment [aviation] is the fastest growing source of greenhouse gases."[63]

— Kenneth Richter, spokesperson for Friends of the Earth.

has started a program of installing solar panels on the roofs of its stores. In addition, new Wal-Mart stores are being designed to take more advantage of natural sunlight, which can help heat the stores as well as cut down on electrical lighting. Eventually, the company hopes to obtain all power for its stores from renewable resources. By early 2009 the company had converted 18 stores and 2 warehouses in Hawaii and California to solar energy and planned to

A Town with Few Cars

The community of Vauban, Germany, has virtually given up cars. Most of the town's 5,000 residents ride bicycles, walk, or take public transportation to school or work. If people need a car to drive out of town, they can join a car-sharing club. As a result, some 70 percent of the town's residents do not own cars. Those who have elected to keep their cars must pay for parking spaces in front of their homes, which cost about $40,000 each.

Vauban is a newly built community—it was completed in 2006. Town planners designed the community, which covers just 1 square mile (2.59 sq. km), to be free of cars; instead of a lot of streets and intersections, there is a generous amount of parks and other green spaces.

In America some state legislatures have adopted tax incentives and similar enticements to create car-free communities. Near Oakland, California, a car-free community known as Quarry Village is in the planning stages. The village will be located adjacent to the California State University in Hayward, giving students, faculty members, and other university employees a place where they can live free of most vehicular traffic. Says David Goldberg, an official of Transportation for America, a group promoting car-free communities, "All of our development since World War II has been centered on the car, and that will have to change."

Quoted in Elisabeth Rosenthal, "In German Suburb, Life Goes On Without Cars," *New York Times*, May 12, 2009, p. A-1.

convert another 20 California stores by the end of 2009. Kim Saylors-Laster, Wal-Mart's vice president of energy, says the initial conversions were regarded as a pilot program, which has now led the company into a full-fledged project to convert all its facilities to solar. Wal-Mart owns some 3,500 stores in the United States as well as about 1,300 in foreign countries.

Officials from Wal-Mart said they have made a commitment to solar both to reduce the company's output of greenhouse gases and to save money. So far, Wal-Mart's commitment to solar power has reduced the company's greenhouse gas output to the equivalent of what 4,000 automobiles produce a year. As for savings, the company believes it will eventually be spending less money for electricity made through solar energy than through fossil fuels. "The pilot program led us to the point that we believe in solar,"[60] says Saylors-Laster.

Another company that has covered its roof with solar panels is Alvah Bushnell Inc. of Philadelphia, one of the country's oldest manufacturers of file folders and similar office products. The company has prospered over the years, but lately it has faced stiff competition from foreign competitors that are able to make folders for less money because they have lower labor costs. To stay competitive, company officials looked at ways to cut costs and decided that their utility bills could be slashed by converting to solar energy. Before converting to solar, the 30,000-square-foot factory (2,787 sq. m) paid about $4,000 a month in electric bills. Since converting to solar, the company has cut its monthly electric bill to about $1,200. Said Andrew Kleeman, the contractor who installed the solar panels on the Bushnell factory roof, "The current generation of Bushnells is certainly proving to be every bit as innovative as the founder."[61]

Flying on Biofuels

Despite the best efforts by individuals as well as large companies, many experts realize that there is simply no way to eliminate a carbon footprint completely from people's lifestyles—at least not with the technology that is currently available. For example, there is no way to travel by air that does not burn fossil fuels—experts have calculated that airlines are responsible for 3 percent of all carbon emissions in the world. However, some airlines, including Continental, Virgin Atlantic, Japan Airlines, and Air New Zealand, have started experimenting with biofuels.

In 2008 Virgin Atlantic made an experimental flight using biofuel rather than oil-based jet fuel. Virgin Atlantic's experimental flight traveled from London to Amsterdam using fuel composed partly of extracts from coconuts and Brazilian nuts. Algae has also been used as a component of biofuels used for aviation. "This pioneering flight will enable those of us who are serious about reducing our carbon emissions to go on developing the fuels of the future,"[62] insisted Richard Branson, the head of Virgin Atlantic.

Environmentalists were less enthusiastic about the test flights, predicting that airlines would eventually conclude that biofuels are too expensive to mass-produce for aviation use. Environmentalists said they would rather see people take fewer flights. "What we need to do is stop this mad expansion of aviation," argued Kenneth Richter, a spokesperson for Friends of the Earth. "At the moment [aviation] is the fastest growing source of greenhouse gases."[63]

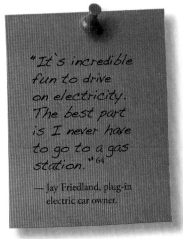

"It's incredible fun to drive on electricity. The best part is I never have to go to a gas station."[64]

— Jay Friedland, plug-in electric car owner.

As airline executives and environmentalists spar over the viability of jet fuel made out of vegetable oil, others call on air travelers to find ways to conserve elsewhere so that they are at least offsetting the impact of jet travel. Perhaps somebody planning a flight can give up driving to work for a few weeks and take a bus instead; or perhaps the traveler can shop for locally produced food so that he or she will not be consuming food that has to be trucked hundreds of miles or even shipped by air or sea for thousands of miles.

A Practical Electric Car

Environmentalists may question whether jets will ever be able to fly without fossil fuels, but the day when cars are able to operate without gasoline is believed to be in the near future. Already, many car manufacturers have produced hybrids—cars that run on a combination of internal combustion engines and electric motors. In some hybrids, which are known as parallel hybrids, the electric motor and gasoline-powered engine work at the same time, each delivering power to the car's transmission, which transfers the power to the wheels. In a series hybrid the gasoline engine powers a generator that is constantly recharging batteries that power the electric motor. It is the electric motor that drives the transmission, and therefore the gasoline-powered engine never directly runs the car.

Experts believe that soon, plug-in electric cars will be widely available to consumers. Already, a few thousand have been sold on a trial basis. These are cars that run entirely on electricity. When they are not in use, their batteries are recharged by plugging the car into ordinary house current. The challenge to automakers will be to develop batteries that can last a long time. At the present time, most batteries need to be recharged after 50 miles (80km) or so of driving.

There is actually nothing new about the concept of running cars on batteries. In 1900 a third of all new cars made in America ran on batteries. That statistic may sound impressive, but in 1900—in the era before Henry Ford perfected the techniques of mass production—only about 4,000 cars a year were manufactured by American automakers. The others ran on steam power and the internal combustion engine.

Battery power did not last any longer in the early 1900s than it does today, but few car owners had to worry about driving their vehicles for more than 50 miles (80km) at a time. There were few paved roads, and therefore there were not many places to drive. Of course, that would change in the coming decades as streets and roads were paved with concrete and asphalt.

In those early years of the auto industry, the internal combustion engine was not a popular choice among car owners, mostly because cars powered by gasoline-fired engines were difficult to start. The driver had to hand crank the engine in order to get it to kick on. Getting the car to start took strong biceps; cranking the engine was unwieldy, difficult, and often unsuccessful. In 1912, though, the inventor Charles Kettering introduced an advancement that would revolutionize the car business—he perfected an electric starter motor that would do the job of the hand crank. Now all a driver had to do was throw an ignition switch inside the car and the gas-powered engine came to life. That advancement helped make the internal combustion engine the dominant source of power in the auto industry, soon killing steam-powered cars as well as all-electric vehicles.

Research Continues

Over the next several decades, manufacturers would tinker with the concept of the electric car, but none were mass-produced until 1997, when the Japanese automaker Toyota introduced the Prius, a hybrid that sold 18,000 cars in its first year. Other manufacturers soon introduced their own hybrids, and today it is estimated that about a million hybrids have been sold in America. Clearly, hybrids are popular, and there is no questioning their high fuel efficiency. In 2009 the hybrid Ford Fusion, regarded as one of the most fuel-efficient models on the market, was rated at 41 miles per gallon (17.43km/L) in city driving—well above the Corporate Average Fuel Economy ratings mandated by Congress.

Meanwhile, research continues on plug-ins—already, a few have been produced on an experimental basis for a handful of owners. Jay Friedland, a California man, owns a plug-in built by

Ford Motor Company shows off its 2010 Fusion hybrid sedan at the 2009 Denver Auto Show. The Fusion has been rated as one of the most fuel-efficient cars on the market.

Powering Japan on Cooking Oil

Many Japanese people love to eat tempura, which is a seafood and vegetable dish. To make tempura, the ingredients are fried in soybean oil. Japanese households and restaurants throw away an estimated 200,000 tons (181,437 metric tons) of used soybean oil each year.

Now entrepreneurs in Japan have found ways to collect the used oil and refine it into biodiesel. Called vegetable diesel fuel, the concoction does not emit greenhouse gases. Yumi Someya, an executive with U Corporation, a Japanese company that collects the used soybean oil from restaurants and homeowners, says her company has signed contracts to sell the fuel to Tokyo's city bus company as well as local trucking companies. In 2009 U Corporation sold the soybean-based fuel at about $4 a gallon, making it competitive with the prices charged for oil-based diesel fuel. As for getting the soybean oil to make the biodiesel fuel, Someya says there is no shortage of tempura lovers in Tokyo who are willing to sell their used oil. "Tokyo is a big oil field," she says, "and every home and restaurant is a spot for drilling."

Quoted in Yuki Oda, "Turning Japan's Used Cooking Oil into Clean Fuel," *Time*, October 5, 2009, p. 48.

Toyota. "It's incredible fun to drive on electricity," says Friedland. "The best part is I never have to go to a gas station."[64]

One of the challenges for automakers is to find places where car owners can charge their batteries away from home. Some manufacturers have proposed to establish charging spots, which are places on the street where an electric car owner can park and plug in the car to obtain a charge. Manufacturers suggest the posts will resemble parking meters. A drawback of this concept is that it could take several hours to recharge the batteries—so the car owner has to be prepared to wait. Other manufacturers have proposed battery swap stations, where fresh batteries can be inserted into cars. Under this concept the manufacturer would actually own the batteries, and the car owner could have fresh batteries installed for a fee whenever necessary. A drawback to this concept is that all the cars would have to be engineered to accept batteries of the same size. Otherwise, a Ford plug-in would not be able to have its battery replaced at a Chevrolet swap station.

Another major issue is that once plug-ins become available, the charge in the battery is not likely to last for more than 100 miles (161km). This means electric cars would be impractical for long trips—the driver would have to look for a swap station or recharging post every 100 miles, which could occur after less than two hours of driving. Nevertheless, manufacturers push on. The French automaker Renault has signed an agreement with a California-based company, Better Place, to provide recharging posts and swap stations for a plug-in that Renault plans to introduce soon. Better Place is establishing a network of posts and swap stations in Israel, Australia, and Denmark and is expected to have the network in operation by 2011. Better Place intends to launch similar networks in Hawaii and California a year later. Shai Agassi, the chief executive officer of Better Place, says the network can be made available to other automakers as long as they engineer their cars to recharge or swap batteries at the facilities designed by Better Place. "Until now, nobody produced these cars so there was no energy network in place," says Agassi. "But if you don't set up a network, nobody buys the cars."[65]

> "Until now, nobody produced these cars so there was no energy network in place. But if you don't set up a network, nobody buys the cars."[65]
>
> — Shai Agassi, chief executive officer of a California company establishing recharging stations for electric cars.

Untapped Potential

If Agassi and other entrepreneurs can establish their networks, it is not inconceivable that in a short time some countries will reduce their dependence on fossil fuels to negligible amounts. Iceland generates 80 percent of its energy from renewable resources, mostly hydroelectric and geothermal power. Geothermal is very important in Iceland because of the country's unique geographical position of sitting atop some of the most significant geothermal resources on the planet. Already, geothermal provides about 25 percent of Iceland's energy needs, including 90 percent of its energy for heating and hot water. In one geothermal project in Iceland,

Like many U.S. cities, Austin, Texas, suffers from gridlock during peak travel hours. Despite increasing popularity of alternative-fuel vehicles, most of the 250 million cars on American roadways are powered by carbon-emitting internal combustion engines.

engineers have bored 2 miles (3.2km) down into a volcano to tap the energy underground.

This reservoir of abundant and clean energy promises to change Iceland from a tiny island nation whose economy has been based mostly on fishing into something of a manufacturing giant. Alcoa, the huge American aluminum manufacturing company, has recently built a $1.5 billion plant in Iceland. Alcoa was drawn to Iceland out of fear that building the plant in the United States would mean relying on fossil fuels for energy, which the company expects to skyrocket in price in the coming years.

In Spain wind turbines dot the landscape, taking advantage of the strong air currents that blow across the Iberian Peninsula. Wind power provides 16 percent of the country's energy, with other renewable resources contributing about 14 percent. Spain has ambitious plans to develop offshore wind stations, taking advantage of the strong air currents that blow along the country's 5,000-mile coastline (8,000km). These turbines would stand on the seafloor, rising high above the surface of the water. Experts believe Spain's offshore stations could generate energy equivalent to what could be produced by 6 nuclear power plants.

All of these projects and many others like them give hope to environmentalists that world leaders have finally recognized the dangers of global warming and have made commitments to change society so that people can find ways to exist without oil, coal, and gas. Perhaps people do not have to live as the Beavans chose to do, but if they can drive electric cars, live in homes powered by wind farms, and work in factories or offices powered by solar and geothermal energy, they can go a long way toward living in a world free of fossil fuels.

Still, it is likely to be a long time before any of that happens. There are, after all, 250 million cars running on American roads, and 249 million of them are powered entirely by carbon-emitting internal combustion engines. Meanwhile, factory smokestacks belch out greenhouse gases, and coal-fired electric plants leave behind tons of toxic ash. At this point renewable resources such as wind, solar, and geothermal may have a lot of potential, but much of that potential remains untapped.

- According to a study by the United Nations, the average American generates 22 tons (20 metric tons) of carbon dioxide a year—about four times the amount generated by the average resident of all other countries on the planet combined.

- The British airline Silverjet has added a $28 assessment on every ticket; the company donates the money to renewable energy projects as a way of offsetting the fossil fuel use of its planes.

- Several environmentally conscious rock bands have bought carbon offsets on the international cap-and-trade market as a way of making up for their extensive jet travel while touring. Among these bands are the Dave Matthews Band and Barenaked Ladies. Others that have bought offsets to make up for air travel are Ben & Jerry's Ice Cream and the Middlebury (Vermont) College ski team.

- Wangari Maathai, the Kenyan environmentalist who won the 2004 Nobel Peace Prize, has proposed that the world's citizens commit to planting 1 billion trees, which would absorb some 250 million tons (226.8 million metric tons) of carbon dioxide emitted into the atmosphere each year.

- A company named Tesla Motors has developed a plug-in electric sports car that can travel 244 miles (393km) on a single charge; the company charges $109,000 for the car.

- By 2009 there were only about 2,000 plug-in electric cars operating on American roads.

- By 2012 the carmakers Mitsubishi, Chrysler, Ford, and Toyota all expect to introduce plug-in electric cars for sale to consumers.

Related Organizations

American Petroleum Institute (API)

1220 L St. NW
Washington, DC 20005-4070
phone: (202) 682-8000
Web site: www.api.org

A trade organization representing oil and gas companies, API contends that fossil fuels are vital sources of energy. Visitors to the API Web site can download *Climate Challenge: A Progress Report*, which details the industry's efforts to reduce greenhouse gas emissions from fossil fuels.

American Solar Energy Society

2400 Central Ave., Suite A
Boulder, CO 80301
phone: (303) 443-3130
fax: (303) 443-3212
e-mail: ases@ases.org
Web site: www.ases.org

The American Solar Energy Society promotes solar energy use in America. Visitors to the organization's Web site can download articles from the society's magazine, *Solar Today*, which profiles individuals who are dedicated to solar energy. The magazine also features news about developments in the solar energy industry.

American Wind Energy Association

1501 M St. NW, Suite 1000
Washington, DC 20005
phone: (202) 383-2500

fax: (202) 383-2505
e-mail: windmail@awea.org
Web site: www.awea.org

The American Wind Energy Association is the trade organization for manufacturers and installers of wind turbines. Students who visit the organization's Web site can download copies of *Wind Energy Weekly*, the association's weekly newsletter, as well as fact sheets that provide statistics on wind energy use in America.

Geothermal Energy Association
209 Pennsylvania Ave. SE
Washington, DC 20003
phone: (202) 454-5261
fax: (202) 454-5265
e-mail: daniela@geo-energy.org
Web site: www.geo-energy.org

The Geothermal Energy Association is the trade organization representing companies that seek and develop geothermal energy resources. Visitors to the organization's Web site can find information on active geothermal energy projects in Alaska, California, Hawaii, Idaho, Nevada, New Mexico, and Utah.

Institute for Energy Research
1415 S. Voss Rd., Suite 110-287
Houston, TX 77057
phone: (713) 974-1918
fax: (713) 974-1993
Web site: http://instituteforenergyresearch.org

The Institute for Energy Research argues that the climate change threat has been blown out of proportion and that enacting restrictions on fossil fuel use could lead to economic disaster. Visitors to the institute's Web site can find many resources backing its positions as well as histories of coal, oil, and natural gas and how they have contributed to the development of the nation.

Intergovernmental Panel on Climate Change (IPCC)
World Meteorological Organization
7bis(cq) Avenue de la Paix

C.P. 2300, CH-1211
Geneva 2, Switzerland
phone: +41-22-730-8208/54/84
fax: +41-22-730-8025/13
e-mail: IPCC-SEC@wmo.int
Web site: www.ipcc.ch

The IPCC, an international organization that monitors global warming, has compiled scientific studies supporting its assertion that fossil fuels contribute to climate change. By visiting the organization's Web site, students can download copies of the panel's reports and read news updates about international efforts to reduce greenhouse gas emissions.

Organization of the Petroleum Exporting Countries (OPEC)

Obere Donaustrasse 93
A-1020 Vienna, Austria
phone: +43-1 21112-279
Web site: www.opec.org

OPEC is composed of the dozen countries that control two-thirds of the world's oil. OPEC sets production quotas, which have a widespread impact on the availability and price of oil. Students can find a number of resources about oil and its availability on the OPEC Web site, including a downloadable version of the book *World Oil Outlook*.

Rainforest Action Network

221 Pine St., 5th Floor
San Francisco, CA 94104
phone: (415) 398-4404
fax: (415) 398-2732
e-mail: answers@ran.org
Web site: http://ran.org

The environmental group originally organized activities to protect the Amazon rain forest but has expanded its role into working for environmental causes in America. By following the link on the network's Web site to "Global Warming," students can learn how deforestation of tropical jungles contributes to climate change.

Stop Global Warming

15332 Antioch St., No. 168
Pacific Palisades, CA 90272
phone: (310) 454-5726
Web site: www.stopglobalwarming.org

This group promotes efforts to reduce greenhouse gas emissions. By following the link to "Classroom," visitors to the organization's Web site can find many resources specifically designed for students, including the "Down to Earth Guide to Global Warming."

U.S. Department of Energy (DOE)

1000 Independence Ave. SW
Washington, DC 20585
phone: (202) 586-5000
fax: (202) 586-4403
e-mail: The.Secretary@hq.doe.gov
Web site: www.energy.gov

The DOE monitors energy use in America and finances projects that expand the use of renewable resources. By following the "Environment" link on the agency's Web site, students can read about climate change as well as the federal programs designed to reduce carbon emissions.

U.S. Environmental Protection Agency (EPA)

Ariel Rios Building
1200 Pennsylvania Ave. NW
Washington, DC 20460
phone: (202) 272-0167
Web site: www.epa.gov

The EPA is the federal government's chief watchdog over the environment and is responsible for monitoring carbon emissions. Students who visit the EPA's Web site can learn about climate change by following the "Learn the Issues" link. The agency provides a background on the science of global warming.

World Energy Council

5th Floor, Regency House
1-4 Warwick St.
London W1B 5LT
United Kingdom
phone: (+44 20) 7734 5996
fax: (+44 20) 7734 5926
e-mail: info@worldenergy.org
Web site: www.worldenergy.org

The World Energy Council monitors energy use throughout the world and assesses the availability of fossil fuel resources. By following the link for "Publications" on the council's Web site, students can find many reports detailing the size of fossil fuel reserves as well as the advancements made in wind, solar, and geothermal resources.

For Further Research

Books

Colin Beavan, *No Impact Man*. New York: Farrar, Straus and Giroux, 2009.

Michael Brune, *Coming Clean: Breaking America's Addiction to Coal and Oil*. San Francisco: Sierra Club, 2008.

Dan Chiras, *The Homeowner's Guide to Renewable Energy: Achieving Energy Independence Through Solar, Wind, Biomass, and Hydropower*. Gabriola Island, BC: New Society, 2006.

Newt Gingrich, *Drill Here, Drill Now, Pay Less*. Washington, DC: Regnery, 2008.

Al Gore, *An Inconvenient Truth*. New York: Rodale, 2006.

Periodicals

Abby Goodnough, "Turning to Windmills, but Resistance Lingers," *New York Times*, September 13, 2009.

Michael Grunwald, "The Clean Energy Scam," *Time*, April 7, 2008.

Elizabeth Kolbert, "The Catastrophist: NASA's Climate Expert Delivers the News No One Wants to Hear," *New Yorker*, June 29, 2009.

Christopher Mims, "Iceland's Power Down Below," *Popular Science*, July 2009.

Clive Thompson, "Batteries Not Included," *New York Times Magazine*, April 19, 2009.

Web Sites

Electric Car Dreams (www.pbs.org/now/shows/544/index.html). The companion Web site to the PBS *Now* telecast "Electric

Car Dreams" examines the history of electric cars and whether they provide a viable alternative to automobiles powered by internal combustion engines.

The Global Warming Debate (www.pbs.org/newshour/indepth_coverage/science/globalwarming/index.html). Companion Web site to the PBS *NewsHour* telecast "The Global Warming Debate," which examines the science of climate change and whether global warming is caused by fossil fuels.

Kyoto Protocol (http://unfccc.int/kyoto_protocol/items/2830.php). Maintained by the United Nations Framework Convention on Climate Change, the Web site provides the terms of the Kyoto Protocol.

Renewable and Alternative Fuels (www.eia.doe.gov/fuelrenewable.html). The Web site, maintained by the U.S. Energy Information Administration, provides statistics on renewable energy usage in America.

Saved by the Sun (www.pbs.org/wgbh/nova/solar). Companion Web site to the PBS *NOVA* telecast "Saved by the Sun," an overview of the science behind photovoltaic cells.

Source Notes

Introduction: The Consequences of Fossil Fuel Use

1. Quoted in Shaila Dewan, "Tennessee Ash Flood Larger than Initial Estimate," *New York Times*, December 27, 2008, p. A-10.

2. Quoted in Elizabeth Kolbert, "The Catastrophist: NASA's Climate Expert Delivers the News No One Wants to Hear," *New Yorker*, June 29, 2009, p. 39.

3. Quoted in Zachary R. Dowdy, "Obama: U.S. Will Fight Climate Change," *Newsday*, September 23, 2009, p. A-6.

4. Newt Gingrich, *Drill Here, Drill Now, Pay Less*. Washington, DC: Regnery, 2008, p. 52.

5. Quoted in Ken Ward Jr., "EPA Releases Big New Report on Toxic Coal Ash," *Charleston Gazette*, October 27, 2009. http://blogs.wvgazette.com.

6. Quoted in CBS News, "Coal Ash: 130 Million Tons of Waste," October 4, 2009. www.cbsnews.com.

Chapter One: What Are the Origins of the Controversy over Fossil Fuels?

7. Mark Hertsgaard, "Will We Run Out of Gas?" *Time*, November 8, 1999. www.time.com.

8. Intergovernmental Panel on Climate Change, *Climate Change 2007: Synthesis Report*, p. 30. www.ipcc.ch.

9. Barack Obama, "Remarks by the President at United Nations Secretary General Ban Ki-Moon's Climate Change Summit," September 22, 2009. www.whitehouse.gov.

10. U.S. Department of State, *Background Note: Saudi Arabia*, January 2009. www.state.gov.

11. Quoted in Ronald E. Hester and Roy M. Harrison, eds., *Sustainability and Environmental Impact of Energy Sources.* Cambridge, England: Royal Society of Chemistry, 2003, p. 1.

12. Quoted in Auto Channel, "George Washington Carver and Henry Ford Shared a Bio-Fuel Vision," February 18, 2007. www.theautochannel.com.

Chapter Two: How Practical Is Renewable Energy?

13. Quoted in Suzette Parmley, "'Cash for Clunkers' Is in the Books; Dealers and Buyers Beat the Clock While Enduring Computer Glitches Near the End of the Popular Government Trade-In Program," *Philadelphia Inquirer*, August 25, 2009, p. D-1.

14. Quoted in Charles Herman, "'Cash for Clunkers' Environmental Benefits Are in Doubt," ABC News, August 24, 2009. http://abcnews.go.com.

15. Robert L. Bradley Jr., "Renewable Energy: Not Cheap, Not 'Green,'" *Policy Analysis*, Cato Institute, August 27, 1997. www.cato.org.

16. Jay Inslee and Bracken Hendricks, *Apollo's Fire: Igniting America's Clean Energy Economy.* Washington, DC: Island, 2008, p. 86.

17. Quoted in Abby Goodnough, "Turning to Windmills, but Resistance Lingers," *New York Times*, September 13, 2009, p. A-25.

18. Quoted in Goodnough, "Turning to Windmills, but Resistance Lingers."

19. Jay Leno, "Blowin' in the Wind," *Popular Mechanics*, September 2007, p. 46.

20. Quoted in Michael Grunwald, "The Clean Energy Scam," *Time*, April 7, 2008, p. 40.

21. Quoted in David Biello, "Grass Makes Better Ethanol than Corn Does," *Scientific American*, January 8, 2008. www.scientificamerican.com.

22. Gingrich, *Drill Here, Drill Now, Pay Less*, p. 6.

23. Quoted in Matthew L. Wald, "Stimulus Money Puts Clean Coal Projects on a Faster Track," *New York Times*, March 17, 2009, p. B-1.

24. Michael Brune, *Coming Clean: Breaking America's Addiction to Oil and Coal.* San Francisco: Sierra Club, 2008, pp. 44–45.

25. Bracken Hendricks, *Wired for Progress: Building a National Clean-Energy Smart Grid*, Center for American Progress, February 2009, p. 3. www.americanprogress.org.

26. Hendricks, *Wired for Progress*, p. 5.

Chapter Three: How Affordable Is Renewable Energy?

27. Bradley, "Renewable Energy."

28. CNN, "Billionaire Oilman Backs Wind Power," May 19, 2008. www.cnn.com.

29. Quoted in Dan Reed, "Texas Oilman T. Boone Pickens Wants to Supplant Oil with Wind," *USA Today*, July 8, 2008. www.usatoday.com.

30. Quoted in Reed, "Texas Oilman T. Boone Pickens Wants to Supplant Oil with Wind."

31. Quoted in Reed, "Texas Oilman T. Boone Pickens Wants to Supplant Oil with Wind."

32. Quoted in John Porretto, "Pickens Calls Off Massive Wind Farm in Texas," *Boston Globe*, July 8, 2009, p. B-11.

33. Quoted in Elizabeth Souder, "Pickens Paring Down Wind Farm Project," *Dallas Morning News*, July 6, 2009. www.dallasnews.com.

34. Quoted in Andrew Maykuth, "PSE&G Plan Takes Solar Energy Public," *Philadelphia Inquirer*, July 30, 2009, p. A-10.

35. Quoted in Maykuth, "PSE&G Plan Takes Solar Energy Public," p. A-10.

36. Quoted in Rebecca Smith, "New Jersey Outshines 48 of Its Peers in Solar Power," *Wall Street Journal*, July 31, 2009, p. A-5.

37. Quoted in Dan Kelly, "Array of Sunshine: Windsor Township Couple Invest in a Dozen Solar Panels, Cite Environment, Expiring Electric Rate Caps in Move," *Reading Eagle*, June 25, 2009. http://readingeagle.com.

38. Quoted in Sacha Pfeiffer, "'Green Mortgages' Taking Root; Loans That Push Energy Efficiency Could Make Homes More Affordable," *Boston Globe*, November 15, 2007, p. C-1.

39. Quoted in Jeannette J. Lee, "White House Energy Plans Could Anger Enviros," *National Journal*, March 14, 2009, p. 7.

40. Quoted in CNBC, "Pickens Sticks with $150 Oil; Could Fall to $100," July 8, 2008. www.cnbc.com.

Chapter Four: What Policies Should Guide Renewable Energy's Future?

41. Quoted in Terry McSweeney, "Northern California Home to Largest Geothermal Field," KGO-7, San Francisco, November 2, 2007. http://abclocal.go.com.

42. Quoted in McSweeney, "Northern California Home to Largest Geothermal Field."

43. Quoted in Paul Tolme, "Universities Lead the Charge to Mine the Heat Beneath Our Feet," *Climate Edu*, National Wildlife Federation, September 20, 2008. www.nwf.org.

44. Quoted in Stephen Koff, "'70s Policies On Target, Some Experts Contend," *Cleveland Plain Dealer*, October 2, 2005, p. A-1.

45. Quoted in *Economist*, "Bright Prospects," March 10, 2007, p. 22.

46. Dennis Kucinich, "Dennis Kucinich Lays Out Why He Voted Against Clean Energy Act," *Cleveland Leader*, June 27, 2009. www.clevelandleader.com.

47. Damon Moglen, "Why Greenpeace Can't Support Waxman-Markey," Greenpeace, May 29, 2009. http://members.green peace.org.

48. Quoted in John M. Broder, "Adding Something for Everyone, House Leaders Gained a Climate Bill," *New York Times*, July 1, 2009, p. A-20.

49. Quoted in Ben Geman, "House Dems Settle on 15 Percent Renewable Energy Target," *New York Times*, May 13, 2009. www.nytimes.com.

50. Quoted in CNN, "Clinton Hails Global Warming Pact," December 11, 1997. www.cnn.com.

51. Quoted in Associated Press, "Bush: Kyoto Treaty Would Hurt Economy," MSNBC, June 30, 2005. www.msnbc.msn.com.

52. Quoted in Elizabeth Kolbert, "Leading Causes," *New Yorker*, October 5, 2009, p. 23.

53. Quoted in Kolbert, "Leading Causes," p. 23.

54. Quoted in Gaurav Singh, Bloomberg News, "China, India Reach Deal to Reduce Gas Emissions," *Philadelphia Inquirer*, October 22, 2009, p. A-4.

55. Quoted in Kolbert, "Leading Causes," p. 23.

Chapter Five: Can People Live Without Fossil Fuels?

56. Quoted in ABC News, "Excerpt: 'No Impact Man,' by Colin Beavan," September 3, 2009. http://abcnews.go.com.

57. Sandy Bauers, "The Year of Living Without," *Philadelphia Inquirer*, November 8, 2009, p. H-11.

58. Quoted in Clayton Sandell, "Reducing Your Carbon Footprint," ABC News, June 7, 2006. http://abcnews.go.com.

59. Quoted in Sandell, "Reducing Your Carbon Footprint."

60. Quoted in Paul Davidson, "Wal-Mart to Double Amount of Solar Energy Use," *USA Today*, April 21, 2009. www.usatoday.com.

61. Quoted in Diane Mastrull, "A Solar Investment," *Philadelphia Inquirer*, November 15, 2009, p. C-6.

62. Quoted in BBC News, "Airline in First Biofuel Flight," February 24, 2008. http://news.bbc.co.uk.

63. Quoted in BBC News, "Airline in First Biofuel Flight."

64. Quoted in *Weekly Reader News*, "Power Surge!" April 24, 2009, p. 4.

65. Quoted in J. Scott Orr and Brooke Lea Foster, "Making Electric Cars Practical," *Parade*, October 11, 2009, p. 6.

Index

About the Author

Hal Marcovitz, a former newspaper reporter, has written more than 150 books for young readers. Marcovitz and his wife, Gail, have recently installed photovoltaic and solar thermal systems on the roof of their home in Chalfont, Pennsylvania.